"As someone who ha_____ on the Holy Spirit, I _____, ing compiled into a book. He uses God's Word in a simple, straightforward way to help remove the shroud of misunderstanding that often accompanies discussions about the Holy Spirit.

The understanding we have gained about the role of the Holy Spirit in our lives has been invaluable to my wife and me both personally and in ministry. We have been equipped to lead the teens in our ministry towards a more intimate relationship with their Creator through a daily walk with the Holy Spirit. The students have been encouraged and empowered by knowing that there is a Helper who lives within them ready and able to battle the spiritual warfare they so often face. We can literally see a visceral reaction when they come to understand the gift Jesus left for us, and within us, in the person of the Holy Spirit."

Tracy Taylor
Co-Founder and Chairman of the Board
LifeTree Legacies

"I was blessed to participate in Roy's teaching on the Holy Spirit and can't say enough about the breakthrough I experienced in my faith. The result wasn't just life-changing; it was life-giving!

Transformation is the best word I can think of to describe how my life changed once I understood the invitation of the Holy Spirit at a greater level. Truly, that moment was the spark that changed the fire in my heart for ministry. It's a fire that the Holy Spirit is kindling in me daily, and the flames continue to grow bigger as I learn to lean in to the transformation!"

Connie Hougland
Senior Vice President, Ministry Services
National Christian Foundation—Heartland

"It wasn't long after I met Roy that I realized the peace in his life and the power in his teaching came directly from the Holy Spirit. Over the years, Roy has strategically used Scripture and personal stories to teach my wife and me what it means to walk in step with the Holy Spirit and why it is critical, especially as ministry leaders, to be equipped and empowered in this way.

The teaching in this book has given me the freedom I needed to walk purposefully in my identity and work faithfully in my calling. It's essential in our ministry to be able to teach others how to listen to the Holy Spirit and how to discern His ways so they can walk purposefully in their identities and work faithfully in their callings, too. That's why I'm excited about this book. I can't wait to share this teaching with those we serve."

Brent Morris
Co-Founder and Executive Director
Art Set Apart

THE HOLY SPIRIT BOOK

Other Titles by Roy Lessin

Drawing Near

Fret Busters

His Footsteps, My Pathway

Jesus, Name Above All Names

Prayers of Promise

Psalm 23

Today is Your Best Day

Books About Roy Lessin

Country Girl Meets City Boy by Char Lessin

Sons from Afar by Jan Markel

> The inspiring story of how Roy, his brother Don, and his orthodox Jewish father came to faith in Christ.

The
HOLY SPIRIT
BOOK

Discovering the Person, the Purpose, and the Power
of the Promised Holy Spirit

ROY LESSIN

set apart

KANSAS CITY

© 2017 Roy Lessin

ISBN 978-0-9983718-0-1

All rights reserved. No part of this publication may be reproduced, distributed, or transmitted in any form or by any means, including photocopying, recording, or other electronic or mechanical methods, without the prior written permission of the publisher, except in the case of brief quotations embodied in critical reviews and certain other non-commercial uses permitted by copyright law.

Churches and other non-commercial interests may reproduce portions of this book without the express written permission of the publisher, provided that the text does not exceed 500 words and that the text is not material quoted from another publisher. When reproducing text from this book, include the following credit line: "From *The Holy Spirit Book*, published by Art Set Apart, Inc. Used by permission."

Scripture quotations marked KJV are taken from the *Holy Bible*, King James Version.

Scripture quotations marked NKJV are taken from the New King James Version. Copyright © 1982 by Thomas Nelson, Inc.

Scripture quotations marked NLT are taken from the *Holy Bible*, New Living Translation, copyright © 1996, 2004, 2007 by Tyndale House Foundation. Used by permission of Tyndale House Publishers, Inc., Carol Stream, Illinois 60188. All rights reserved.

Scripture quotations marked AMP are taken from the Amplified' Bible, © 1954, 1958, 1962, 1964, 1965, 1987 by The Lockman Foundation. Used by permission. (www.lockman.org)

Scripture quotations marked NASB are taken from the NEW AMERICAN STANDARD BIBLE', © Copyright The Lockman Foundation. (www.lockman.org)

Edited by Kristin Morris.
Cover lettering and typography by Douglas Havach.
Cover art created by Brent Morris.

About the art: *By My Spirit* by Brent Morris

- The dove itself symbolizes the promised gift of the Holy Spirit. [Acts 2:38]

- The shape of the dove's wings represent the hands of Jesus who sent us the Holy Spirit [John 16:7], and the color of the wings represent the Holy Spirit being sent with fire. [Matthew 3:11]

- The three metal rings around the art represent the Holy Trinity God the Father, God the Son, and God the Holy Spirit. [1 John 5:7]

Published by Art Set Apart, Inc.
PO Box 9064
Shawnee Mission, KS 66201-9064
www.setapartkc.com

Printed in the United States of America

*W*ith a prayer that the abundant life
which Jesus came to give us,
the fullness of joy that He promised to us,
and the power of the Holy Spirit
that He sent to be upon us,
will be the reality
of every believing heart.

The CONTENTS

Prologue: A Beautiful Life	11
Introduction	13

Section I: The Person of the Holy Spirit

Chapter 1: Who is the Holy Spirit?	17
Chapter 2: The Beauty Maker	27
Chapter 3: Better Than the Very Best Friend	35

Section II: The Purpose of the Holy Spirit

Chapter 4: The Holy Spirit at Work in Us	43
Chapter 5: Walking in the Spirit	53
Chapter 6: The Spirit Against the Flesh	63
Chapter 7: Recognizing the Voice of the Holy Spirit	69

Section III: The Power of the Holy Spirit

Chapter 8: The Importance of Spiritual Power	81
Chapter 9: The Meaning of Spiritual Power	87
Chapter 10: The Results of Spiritual Power	95

Section IV: The Promise of the Holy Spirit

Chapter 11: The Promise for All Believers	107
Chapter 12: One Holy Spirit, Many Ministries	115
Chapter 13: The Fullness of the Holy Spirit	121
Chapter 14: Receiving the Fullness of the Holy Spirit	133
Chapter 15: Expectations	141

Section V: Author Reflections

Chapter 16: Learning the Ways of the Holy Spirit	157
About the Author	170
Recommended Reading	171
Note Pages	172

The PROLOGUE

A Beautiful Life

If I had to describe myself before putting the teachings of this book into practice, I would have to say that I was a struggling Christian. Mustering up the strength and courage to live a beautiful life eluded me. There were times of peace and joy, but overall there was a restlessness in my soul that plagued me.

For many years I had diligently pursued the deep things of God. I loved His Word and studied hard. There were sweet times of hearing the whispers of His voice. There were encounters with the Holy Spirit that will never be forgotten; they kept me in pursuit of knowing God more intimately. But along with my desire to know Him was also a great defect of character in the core of my being: *I doubted His love.* It is hard to even confess that today.

Thankfully, God heard my humble pleas for aid and sent a man to teach me about the will and the ways of the Helper. Roy taught me in simple words what the Bible says about the person, the purpose, and the power of the promised Holy Spirit. His words not only encouraged me, but enlightened me to what was mine to be had all along: FREEDOM and VICTORY.

I will always remember fondly the evening I spent on my knees receiving the most precious gift: *the baptism with the Holy Spirit.* My life was forever changed. A treasure trove of goodness and mercy was poured out over me that night, and it remains with me still.

It was a beautiful moving of the knowledge of God from my head to my heart. There was a new infusion of power and hope that I had never known before. I was filled with the ability to trust implicitly the Father's love for me, and that made all of those castaway fragments of my life become lovely. There was a sweet surrendering of self that went to greater depths than I had ever been able to experience on my own. Out of that surrender came an ever-present awareness of the constant nearness of God.

The Holy Spirit has turned my life's chaos into order, and all that once confused me has now been made clear. Sorrow and pain have been intertwined with beauty and joy, and in the deepest recesses of my heart I can now say that *it is well with my soul.*

COLLEEN MAGNO WOODS
Sartell, Minnesota

The INTRODUCTION

On a warm summer's evening in August of 1961, in a small cabin style home in Southern California, I knelt by a well-worn living room couch and opened up my heart to the goodness of God to me through the Gospel of Jesus Christ. My prayer was simple, and I knew it was a prayer God heard and answered.

On that day, by faith, I received Jesus as my Savior and surrendered my life to Him as my Lord. In kindness and mercy, Jesus sent the Holy Spirit to me, the One who I would come to know as the Comforter…it was He who awakened me, convicted me, revealed Jesus to me, and drew me to the Father's heart. It was the Holy Spirit who made known to me, for the first time, that all was well between my soul and God…*peace had come!*

Since then, the Holy Spirit has been at work within me, faithfully, consistently, lovingly, drawing me closer to the heart of the Father and conforming me to the image of God's Son. Over and over again the Holy Spirit has whispered the Father's loving thoughts to me, opened my eyes to see more glimpses of Jesus' glory, comforted my heart with the assurance that my life is in God's hands, and established me in the purposes and plans of God's will for my life.

How blessed and privileged we are to know the riches of God's grace in our lives. It is because God sent us the gift of His Son, and because His Son sent us the gift of the Holy Spirit that our lives can be telling a new story. There is no better way to live!

May your heart daily be in awe over the beautiful story God is writing in your life.

ROY LESSIN

SECTION I

The PERSON of the HOLY SPIRIT

*The grace of the Lord Jesus Christ,
and the love of God,
and the communion of the Holy Spirit
be with you all. Amen.*

2 CORINTHIANS 13:14 NKJV

CHAPTER 1

WHO IS THE HOLY SPIRIT?

How much can we know about the Holy Spirit?

We can know as much about the Holy Spirit as the Scriptures have revealed to us. There are many things about the *working* of the Holy Spirit that are mysterious and we may not fully understand, but it does not mean that the *person* of the Holy Spirit should be a mystery to us.

The person of the Holy Spirit is especially endearing to the heart of a follower of Jesus Christ. The Scriptures speak of the Holy Spirit in caring, tender ways. His names call us, invite us, and draw us closer to the heart of God.

God is one God in three persons (see 2 Corinthians 13:14, Matthew 3:16-17, Romans 8:9-11, 1 Peter 1:2, John 3:34, Titus 3:4-6). The three persons are God the Father, God the Son, and God the Holy Spirit. They are co-eternal and co-equal. We call these three persons the Holy Trinity or the triune Godhead. The Father honors the Son, and the Son honors the Holy Spirit; the Holy Spirit honors the Son, and the Son honors the

Father. They are in complete harmony and unity with each other. The will of One is the will of All, the love of One is the love of All, and the holiness of One is the holiness of All. As it is written in Revelation 4:8, *"Holy, holy, holy is the Lord God Almighty."*

Jesus proclaimed this truth when He said in Mark 12:29, *"The Lord our God is one Lord."* Jesus also proclaimed in John 10:30, *"I and my Father are one."* Jesus also told us in John 14:16 that the Holy Spirit was the Spirit of Truth and that the Holy Spirit was being sent to us as *"another* Comforter"— the One who is *exactly* like Him. And it was Jesus who told us in Matthew 28:19 to baptize believers in the name of the Father, the Son, and the Holy Spirit.

How can we explain this truth? Many examples have been given to try and help us understand the reality of one God in three distinct persons. Some of these include the example of a single egg having three parts — the shell, the white, and the yoke. Another example is that water can be steam, liquid, or solid. Another is that a man can be a father, a husband, and a son. Although each of these examples help somewhat, they fall far short in helping us understand the depth of the meaning of the triune Godhead. To learn of God is to be in awe of His words, His works, His attributes, and His ways. By faith, each of us can boldly proclaim, "Who is like the Lord our God?"

Can the human really explain the Divine? How can the finite grasp the infinite? How can the limited define the omnipotent? How can the human mind fathom the depth of the all-knowing God? We can't. We are not asked to understand it or explain it, but we can fully believe it!

> *Oh, the depth of the riches both of the wisdom and knowledge of God! How unsearchable are His judgments and His ways past finding out!* ROMANS 11:33 NKJV

Who is the Holy Spirit?

The Bible reveals many other names about each person of the Trinity. These names help us understand more about what each person of the Trinity does, who He is, and how He works. For example, God is called Adonai, which means "The Lord and Master." (He is in charge of my life and has the final say); El Shaddai, which means "The Lord God Almighty." (Nothing is impossible with God, and I can fully trust Him); and El Olam, which means "The Everlasting God." (He is unchanging, and I can rest in His faithfulness). Jesus is called The Way (to the Father), The Savior (from sin), and the Messiah (The Anointed One); the Holy Spirit is called the Comforter (the One who comes alongside), the Spirit of Truth (the One who reveals Scripture to us and testifies of Jesus), and the Sanctifier (the One who separates us unto God).

The Bible uses specific words in Scripture to symbolize the Holy Spirit. These symbolic names also help us understand various aspects of the Holy Spirit's work. The Holy Spirit is likened to a dove in John 1:32, but the Holy Spirit is not "a dove." The Holy Spirit is likened to the wind in Acts 2:2, but the Holy Spirit is not "the wind." The Holy Spirit influences our lives like in John 16:8, but the Holy Spirit is not "an influence."

The divine nature of the Holy Spirit is revealed in His attributes, which are described throughout Scripture.

HE IS ETERNAL.
How much more shall the blood of Christ, who through the eternal Spirit offered Himself without spot to God, cleanse your conscience from dead works to serve the living God?
HEBREWS 9:14 NKJV

HE IS ALL-PRESENT.
Where can I go from Your Spirit? Or where can I flee from Your presence? **PSALM 139:7 NKJV**

HE IS ALL-KNOWING.
> *For the Spirit searches all things, yes, the deep things of God. For what man knows the things of a man except the spirit of the man which is in him? Even so no one knows the things of God except the Spirit of God.* 1 CORINTHIANS 2:10-11 NKJV

HE IS ALL-POWERFUL.
> *For I will not dare to speak of any of those things which Christ has not accomplished through me, in word and deed, to make the Gentiles obedient—in mighty signs and wonders, by the power of the Spirit of God, so that from Jerusalem and round about to Illyricum I have fully preached the gospel of Christ.* ROMANS 15:18-19 NKJV

THE HOLY SPIRIT IS A DIVINE PERSON, NOT AN "IT."

The pronouns used in Scripture refer to the Holy Spirit as a person. For example, when speaking about the Holy Spirit, Jesus said:

> *"When **He**, the Spirit of truth shall come, **He** will guide you into all truth."* JOHN 16:13 KJV

THE HOLY SPIRIT IS THE COUNSELOR.
Jesus refers to the Holy Spirit as the Counselor and not counsel. Counsel is advice, not a person. It takes a counselor to give counsel.

THE HOLY SPIRIT IS THE COMFORTER.
In the same way, Jesus refers to the Holy Spirit as the Comforter and not comfort. It takes a comforter to give comfort.

THE HOLY SPIRIT HAS THE CHARACTERISTICS OF A PERSON.

THE HOLY SPIRIT HAS A MIND.
*Now He who searches the hearts knows what the **mind** of the Spirit is, because He makes intercession for the saints according to the will of God.* ROMANS 8:27 NKJV

THE HOLY SPIRIT HAS A WILL.
*But one and the same Spirit works all these things, distributing to each one individually as **He wills**.*
1 CORINTHIANS 12:11 NKJV

THE HOLY SPIRIT HAS EMOTIONS.
*But they rebelled and **grieved** His Holy Spirit.*
ISAIAH 63:10 NKJV

THE HOLY SPIRIT HAS A VOICE.

HE WARNS.
He who is able to hear, let him listen to and heed what the [Holy] Spirit says to the assemblies (churches).
REVELATION 3:6 AMP

HE GUIDES.
Now when they had gone through Phrygia and the region of Galatia, they were forbidden by the Holy Spirit to preach the word in Asia. ACTS 16:6 NKJV

HE REVEALS SCRIPTURE.
*Men and brethren, this Scripture had to be fulfilled, which the Holy Spirit **spoke** before by the mouth of David.*
ACTS 1:16 NKJV

He prays.

> *And the Holy Spirit helps us in our weakness. For example, we don't know what God wants us to pray for. But the Holy Spirit prays for us with groanings that cannot be expressed in words. And the Father who knows all hearts knows what the Spirit is saying, for the Spirit pleads for us believers in harmony with God's own will.* ROMANS 8:26 NLT

He teaches.

> *But the Helper, the Holy Spirit, whom the Father will send in My name, He will teach you all things, and bring to your remembrance all things that I said to you.* JOHN 14:26 NKJV

He testifies.

> *But when the Helper comes, whom I shall send to you from the Father, the Spirit of truth who proceeds from the Father, He will testify of Me.* JOHN 15:26 NKJV

When the prophet Elijah was taken to heaven in a whirlwind and Elisha took up Elijah's mantle that fell from him (2 Kings 2:1-18), we discover that a group of 50 sons of the prophets witnessed the event at a distance. Although both the sons of the prophets and Elisha knew about the Holy Spirit, the sons of the prophets only knew about the Holy Spirit from afar. Elisha on the other hand, was pressing in to have all of the Holy Spirit that could be his.

After a double portion of the Holy Spirit had come upon Elisha, the sons of the prophets drew near with their concerns. Even though they were familiar with the works of the Holy Spirit, they did not know the Holy Spirit's heart or His ways.

The sons of the prophets thought that since the Holy Spirit was involved in the experience they had just witnessed that something harmful could have happened to Elijah. They were ready to form a search party and rescue Elijah from his peril. They told Elisha, "Perhaps the Spirit of the Lord has taken him up and cast him on some mountain or into some valley." Elisha told them not to go, for Elisha knew that there was nothing to fear about the Holy Spirit, and that He would never abandon God's people or do them harm.

There is no person more wonderful than the Holy Spirit. He is the Spirit of Truth, and He never deceives us, lies to us, bears false witness, or misleads us. He reveals Jesus to us and brings the life of Jesus to us…that is why Jesus sent Him!

My Prayer

Heavenly Father, thank You for being so good to me.

Jesus, thank You for sending the **Holy Spirit** to me, and that He has come to work in me everything that You have done for me. How blessed I am to know that the **Holy Spirit** is a divine person who cares for me, loves me, and teaches me the truth of who You are.

Holy Spirit, thank You for Your presence and the communion I am able to experience with You each day. You are closer to me than anyone, for You dwell within me and will abide with me always.

Show me more and more of **Jesus,** teach me Your heart, guide me in Your ways, lead me in Your truth, establish me in Your righteousness through the power of the **Holy Spirit.**

Amen.

Notes

*Give unto the LORD the glory due to His name;
worship the LORD in the beauty of holiness.*

PSALM 29:2 NKJV

CHAPTER 2

The Beauty Maker

*B*eauty is one of those special "welcoming" words. It's a word we like to invite into our thoughts and set a table for in our hearts. We were made to identify, enjoy, and celebrate beauty. Beauty is something we want to bring into the light so we can look upon it, something we want to bring into our conversation so we can talk about it, and something we want to give to others so they can be blessed by it.

We were made to love beautiful things—beautiful art brings us to museums; beautiful flowers draw us to gardens; beautiful sunsets draw us to the western sky; beautiful music draws us to the symphony hall.

We were made to delight in beauty, and it is the beauty of the Lord that fills us with the greatest of all joys. The Lord invites us to draw close to Him, to look upon His beautiful character, and to examine His ways. The closer we come, the more beauty we see.

In Isaiah 6:3 we read, "*Holy, holy, holy is the Lord of hosts.*" God the Father is holy, Jesus Christ is holy, and the Holy Spirit is holy.

Another way of understanding the word "holy" is "beauty." Each person of the Godhead is beautiful because each person is holy. Their character is beautiful, their nature is beautiful, their ways are beautiful, their attitudes are beautiful, their glory is beautiful, and their presence in our hearts is beautiful.

Every aspect of beauty is found, in its fullness, in God alone. God has no flaws, no stains, no impurities, and no defilement. His holiness allows us to delight in Him, enjoy Him, and behold Him in deep adoration.

Dr. G. Campbell Morgan, the respected British evangelist, preacher, and Bible scholar once said, "The Holy Spirit is the Creator of beauty."

This is what the Bible says about the beauty of God's holiness:

> **HOLINESS** is glorious. [Exodus 15:11]
>
> **HOLINESS** is the true identity of the True God. [Exodus 15:11]
>
> **HOLINESS** guarantees that God's promises are true. [Psalm 89:35]
>
> **HOLINESS** brings the memories that produce thankfulness. [Psalm 97:12]
>
> **HOLINESS** is the garment a warrior wears into victory. [Psalm 110:3]
>
> **HOLINESS** will always lead us in the right direction. [Isaiah 35:8]

The Beauty Maker

> **HOLINESS** is the hand that opens the windows of worship in our souls. [1 Chronicles 16:29]

All of the beautiful things of God are brought to our hearts by the Holy Spirit. The Holy Spirit is our beauty maker. Beauty is found wherever there is truth, wherever there is goodness, wherever there is righteousness, wherever there is love. Jesus sent the Holy Spirit to pour out the beauty of the Lord upon our lives.

> *In that day the LORD of hosts will be for a crown of glory and a diadem of beauty to the remnant of His people.* ISAIAH 28:5 NKJV

The Holy Spirit's beautiful work means He purifies us, sanctifies us, cleanses us, and washes us clean. How beautiful are His ways with us; how beautiful is His work within us as He conforms us to the image of Jesus Christ.

> **The Spirit of the Lord GOD is upon Me**, because the LORD has anointed Me to preach good tidings to the poor; He has sent Me to heal the brokenhearted, to proclaim liberty to the captives, and the opening of the prison to those who are bound; to proclaim the acceptable year of the LORD, and the day of vengeance of our God; to comfort all who mourn, to console those who mourn in Zion, **to give them beauty for ashes**, the oil of joy for mourning, the garment of praise for the spirit of heaviness; that they may be called trees of righteousness, the planting of the LORD, that He may be glorified. ISAIAH 61:1-3 NKJV

The following examples help us to understand the true qualities of beauty in the Holy Spirit and how these qualities are revealed in our lives through His character.

HIS BEAUTY RADIATES.
Every bride is different, yet every bride is beautiful. Whether the wedding is outside or inside, on a mountaintop, or at a beach, all who attend have one expectation…to see the bride. When the bride appears, all eyes are fixed upon her. The setting is important, the wedding dress is important, the bouquet is important, but the place every eye turns is upon the face of the bride. It is her radiance (the beauty from within) that draws the attention of the guests and captures their hearts.

Every child of God who carries the radiance of the Lord upon their countenance is beautiful to look upon.

> *So all of us who have had that veil removed can see and reflect the glory of the Lord. And the Lord—who is the Spirit—makes us more and more like Him as we are changed into His glorious image.* 2 CORINTHIANS 3:18 NLT

HIS BEAUTY ENRICHES.
We don't need to have a big bank account to be rich. The beauty of a Godly character is that it enriches every aspect of our lives. It makes even the poorest person a wealthy person.

The wonderful thing about the beauty of the Lord is that it doesn't diminish within us through the passing years, but rather increases instead. His beauty doesn't bring less to our lives; it brings more. The magnificence of His beauty takes us to higher ground and greater depths of joy. It is the Lord's beauty that deepens our walk with Him and our love for Him.

> *And let the **beauty** of the LORD our God be upon us.*
> PSALM 90:17 NKJV

The Beauty Maker

His beauty purifies.

We enjoy looking at clear skies, breathing air that is not polluted, and walking on pathways that are not covered with litter. We want to swim in untainted oceans, fish in clear lakes, and drink from the purest of streams. The purer the stream, the more lovely its waters, but the purest stream flows from the heart of God.

> *Anyone who believes in Me may come and drink! For the Scriptures declare, "Rivers of living water will flow from his heart."* JOHN 7:38 NLT

My Prayer

Lord, You are beautiful—beautiful in life, in truth, in thoughts, in attitudes, in actions—You are beautiful in character, and Your beauty shines in glorious light. **Holy Spirit**, shine in me the character which chooses the highest good, which demonstrates the deepest love, which maintains the truest course, which extends the kindest manner, and which walks the purest path. I see beauty in all You do and in all Your purposes for my life. I see beauty as You conform me to the image of **Jesus**, and as You work in me everything that is pleasing in **God's** sight. Thank You for the beautiful work You are doing in my life.

AMEN.

Notes

*Nevertheless I tell you the truth.
It is to your advantage that I go away;
for if I do not go away, the Helper will not come to you;
but if I depart, I will send Him to you.*

JOHN 16:7 NKJV

CHAPTER 3

Better Than the Very Best Friend

The Holy Spirit is the One who is exactly like Jesus in His nature and character. When we become believers in Jesus Christ and receive Him as our Lord and Savior, Jesus sends the Holy Spirit to live in us and to be with us always. We have the awesome privilege of spending each day with the Holy Spirit, the perfect companion.

Each of us can be eternally grateful for the ministry of the Holy Spirit. Without Him, none of us would know the love of Jesus Christ, nor be expectantly awaiting His return.

The Holy Spirit is even better than the very best friend, because He is the *HOLY* Spirit—all of His characteristics are expressed in the purest of ways and for the highest purpose.

He is Kind—The Holy Spirit is gentle like a dove.

> *When He had been baptized, Jesus came up immediately from the water; and behold, the heavens were opened to Him, and He saw the Spirit of God descending like a dove and alighting upon Him.* MATTHEW 3:16 NKJV

HE IS LOYAL—The Holy Spirit always directs us into God's will and plan for our lives.

> *As they ministered to the Lord and fasted, the Holy Spirit said, "Now separate to Me Barnabas and Saul for the work to which I have called them."* ACTS 13:2 NKJV

HE IS TRUTHFUL—The Holy Spirit is the Spirit of Truth.

> *But when He, the Spirit of truth, comes, He will guide you into all the truth; for He will not speak on His own initiative, but whatever He hears, He will speak; and He will disclose to you what is to come.* JOHN 16:13 NASB

HE IS HONEST—The Holy Spirit bears witness to everything that is good and right.

> *The Holy Spirit also witnesses to us.* HEBREWS 10:15 NKJV

HE IS DEPENDABLE—The Holy Spirit is always with us and is there for us.

> *You know Him (the Spirit of truth), for He dwells with you and will be in you.* JOHN 14:17 NKJV

HE IS PATIENT—The Holy Spirit waits for His fruit to grow and mature in our lives.

> *But the Holy Spirit produces this kind of fruit in our lives: love, joy, peace, patience, kindness, goodness, faithfulness, gentleness, and self-control. There is no law against these things!* GALATIANS 5:22-23 NLT

HE IS ENCOURAGING—The Holy Spirit is the One who edifies, builds us up, and gives us wise counsel.

> *The Spirit of the LORD shall rest upon Him, The Spirit of wisdom and understanding, The Spirit of counsel and might, The Spirit of knowledge and of the fear of the LORD.* ISAIAH 11:2 NKJV

HE IS HELPFUL—The Holy Spirit is the perfect Helper who comes alongside us to reassure us in every possible way. He helps us in our weakness to stand strong. He helps us to break every yoke in our bondages. He helps us to know the will of God when we pray. He helps us to remember the things Jesus said. And He helps us to keep the hope of better things to come strong within our hearts.

> *But the Helper, the Holy Spirit, whom the Father will send in My name, He will teach you all things, and bring to your remembrance all things that I said to you.* JOHN 14:26 NKJV

HE IS COMFORTING—The Holy Spirit is the tender Comforter. He knows our sorrows and sees our tears. He quiets our troubled hearts and assures us that it is well with our souls. He brings us through the storms of life and guides us to safe harbors. He keeps us in God's perfect peace. And He assures us that we are never alone.

> *Then the churches throughout all Judea, Galilee, and Samaria had peace and were edified. And walking in the fear of the Lord and in the comfort of the Holy Spirit, they were multiplied.* ACTS 9:31 NKJV

HE IS LOVING—The Holy Spirit is the One who fills our hearts with the love of God.

> *Now hope does not disappoint, because the love of God has been poured out in our hearts by the Holy Spirit who was given to us.* ROMANS 5:5 NKJV

Just as we can be assured that the Holy Spirit will *always* express the characteristics mentioned above, we can also be assured that the Holy Spirit will *never* express cruelty, unfaithfulness, deception, unreliability, impatience, discouragement, unhelpfulness, indifference, or hatefulness.

Who could be more assuring than the Comforter, who could be gentler than the Heavenly Dove, or who could be more knowing and wise than the Spirit of Truth? Who else could bring joy to our hearts, light to our pathways, and rest to our innermost beings? Who else could do a better job of pointing us to Jesus, of revealing Scripture to our hearts, and of assuring us of God's eternal love and care? No one but the Holy Spirit.

> "One of the Holy Spirit's most loveable characteristics is that He deliberately submerges Himself in Jesus; He works at being inconspicuous. Always there is a transparency in His personality so that Jesus can shine through."
>
> —CATHERINE MARSHALL

Better Than the Very Best Friend

My Prayer

Thank You, **Holy Spirit**, that You are my tender friend.

You will never ignore me, despise me, or abandon me.

There is no friend like You. You will always encourage me,

teach me, and direct me to do the right thing, the good thing,

the best thing, and the most loving thing...

just like a very best friend. You are gracious and merciful.

You are pure, perfect without flaw, and lack nothing.

Because You are loyal, I can trust You

with every detail of my life.

Deepen my trust, for You are trustworthy;

strengthen my faith, for You are faithful;

cause me to grow in Your love,

for You are altogether lovely.

AMEN

SECTION II

The PURPOSE of the HOLY SPIRIT

⁵Jesus answered, "Most assuredly, I say to you,
unless one is born of water and the Spirit,
he cannot enter the kingdom of God.

⁶That which is born of the flesh is flesh,
and that which is born of the Spirit is spirit.

⁷Do not marvel that I said to you,
'You must be born again.'

⁸The wind blows where it wishes,
and you hear the sound of it,
but cannot tell where it comes from and where it goes.
So is everyone who is born of the Spirit."

JOHN 3:5-8 NKJV

CHAPTER 4

The Holy Spirit at Work in Us

Jesus told us that our spiritual life in God's kingdom begins when we are born again. This spiritual birth takes place at the time we receive Jesus Christ by faith. That's when the Holy Spirit enters into our lives and brings eternal life to our hearts.

> *But as many as received Him, to them He gave the right to become children of God, even to those who believe in His name, who were born, not of blood nor of the will of the flesh nor of the will of man, but of God.* JOHN 1:12-13 NASB

The work of the Holy Spirit in our lives is invaluable, as it is He who makes us truly alive on the inside. Without the Holy Spirit's presence within us, we are spiritually dead. He is the life-giver.

> *And you He made alive, who were dead in trespasses and sins.* EPHESIANS 2:1 NKJV

The Holy Spirit brings to us the life that Jesus provided through His death on the cross, His burial, His resurrection, and His ascension to the right hand of the Father. It is through the Holy Spirit that our lives become the possession of the Lord.

> *Now if anyone does not have the Spirit of Christ, he is not His.* ROMANS 8:9 NKJV

The eighth chapter of Romans is one of the greatest teachings in the Bible on the work of the Holy Spirit in the life of a believer. Consider what the Apostle Paul tells us about the ministry of the Holy Spirit in our lives.

> *¹There is therefore now no condemnation to those who are in Christ Jesus, who do not walk according to the flesh, but according to the Spirit.*
>
> *²For the law of the Spirit of life in Christ Jesus has made me free from the law of sin and death.*
>
> *³For what the law could not do in that it was weak through the flesh, God did by sending His own Son in the likeness of sinful flesh, on account of sin: He condemned sin in the flesh,*
>
> *⁴that the righteous requirement of the law might be fulfilled in us who do not walk according to the flesh but according to the Spirit.*
>
> *⁵For those who live according to the flesh set their minds on the things of the flesh, but those who live according to the Spirit, the things of the Spirit.*
>
> *⁶For to be carnally minded is death, but to be spiritually minded is life and peace.*
>
> *⁷Because the carnal mind is enmity against God; for it is not subject to the law of God, nor indeed can be.*

⁸*So then, those who are in the flesh cannot please God.*

⁹*But you are not in the flesh but in the Spirit, if indeed the Spirit of God dwells in you. Now if anyone does not have the Spirit of Christ, he is not His.*

¹⁰*And if Christ is in you, the body is dead because of sin, but the Spirit is life because of righteousness.*

¹¹*But if the Spirit of Him who raised Jesus from the dead dwells in you, He who raised Christ from the dead will also give life to your mortal bodies through His Spirit who dwells in you.*

¹²*Therefore, brethren, we are debtors—not to the flesh, to live according to the flesh.*

¹³*For if you live according to the flesh you will die; but if by the Spirit you put to death the deeds of the body, you will live.*

¹⁴*For as many as are led by the Spirit of God, these are sons of God.*

¹⁵*For you did not receive the spirit of bondage again to fear, but you received the Spirit of adoption by whom we cry out, "Abba, Father."*

¹⁶*The Spirit Himself bears witness with our spirit that we are children of God,*

¹⁷*and if children, then heirs—heirs of God and joint heirs with Christ, if indeed we suffer with Him, that we may also be glorified together.*

• • •

²³Not only that, but we also who have the firstfruits of the Spirit, even we ourselves groan within ourselves, eagerly waiting for the adoption, the redemption of our body.

²⁴For we were saved in this hope, but hope that is seen is not hope; for why does one still hope for what he sees?

²⁵But if we hope for what we do not see, we eagerly wait for it with perseverance.

²⁶Likewise the Spirit also helps in our weaknesses. For we do not know what we should pray for as we ought, but the Spirit Himself makes intercession for us with groanings which cannot be uttered.

²⁷Now He who searches the hearts knows what the mind of the Spirit is, because He makes intercession for the saints according to the will of God.

ROMANS 8:1-17; 23-27 NKJV

IT IS THE HOLY SPIRIT who speaks with the voice of clarity and truth. His voice never sounds confusing, and He never speaks empty words that have no meaning.

IT IS THE HOLY SPIRIT who keeps us from guessing about our right standing and relationship with God. There is no guesswork with the Holy Spirit.

IT IS THE HOLY SPIRIT who assures us of our security in Christ, who places within us the heart-cry "Abba Father," and who speaks to us as true heirs of the promises of God.

IT IS THE HOLY SPIRIT who testifies to us our freedom from all condemnation, who applies to our hearts the law of liberty provided through Christ's atonement, and who frees us from the power of sin and its consequences.

The Holy Spirit at Work in Us

It is the Holy Spirit who places our feet upon the pathway of peace, who indwells us, who assures us that we are God's children, who brings us the mind of Christ, who leads us to the things that please God, who renews our physical bodies, and who frees us from all bondage and fear.

It is the Holy Spirit who helps us in our weaknesses, who prays for us in our need, who lines up everything in our lives according to the will of God, who puts heaven in our vision, hope in our hearts, and joy in our journeys as He reveals to us our true riches in Christ.

It is the Holy Spirit who tells us, over and over again, that we are the Lord's, that the Father loves us, that God is for us, that He is working all things together for good, and that Jesus is our Savior, our Shepherd, and our coming King.

It is the Holy Spirit who brings the reality of Christ to our hearts, the fellowship of God to our spirits, the light of the Scriptures to our understanding, and who makes the communion we have with other believers possible.

The work of the Holy Spirit never goes out of date, becomes dull or stale, or loses its power. As He worked in the lives of believers in the Bible, so He works in our lives today. His work is and always will be relevant in every generation.

He convicts us of sin and points us to our need of Christ.

> *Nevertheless I tell you the truth. It is to your advantage that I go away; for if I do not go away, the Helper will not come to you; but if I depart, I will send Him to you. And when He has come, He will convict the world of sin, and of righteousness, and of judgment.* JOHN 16:7-8 NKJV

He brings us spiritual life through the new birth.

> *Jesus answered, "Most assuredly, I say to you, unless one is born of water and the Spirit, he cannot enter the kingdom of God. That which is born of the flesh is flesh, and that which is born of the Spirit is spirit. Do not marvel that I said to you, 'You must be born again.'"* JOHN 3:5-7 NKJV

He imparts hope in the good things God has ahead.

> *Now may the God of hope fill you with all joy and peace in believing, that you may abound in hope by the power of the Holy Spirit.* ROMANS 15:13 NKJV

He teaches us the things of God in His classroom of life, for life.

> *But the Helper, the Holy Spirit, whom the Father will send in My name, He will teach you all things, and bring to your remembrance all things that I said to you.* JOHN 14:26 NKJV

He empowers us to serve the Lord.

> *But you shall receive power (ability, efficiency, and might) when the Holy Spirit has come upon you, and you shall be My witnesses in Jerusalem and all Judea and Samaria and to the ends (the very bounds) of the earth.* ACTS 1:8 AMP

He frees us from the power of sin and its controlling hold upon our lives.

> *There is therefore now no condemnation to those who are in Christ Jesus, who do not walk according to the flesh, but according to the Spirit. For the law of the Spirit of life in Christ Jesus has made me free from the law of sin and death.* ROMANS 8:1-2 NKJV

The Holy Spirit at Work in Us

He intercedes for us with passion and compassion in our prayer life.

> *Likewise the Spirit also helps in our weaknesses. For we do not know what we should pray for as we ought, but the Spirit Himself makes intercession for us with groanings which cannot be uttered. Now He who searches the hearts knows what the mind of the Spirit is, because He makes intercession for the saints according to the will of God.*
> ROMANS 8:26-27 NKJV

He makes known to us what is in the heart of God.

> *But as it is written: "Eye has not seen, nor ear heard, nor have entered into the heart of man the things which God has prepared for those who love Him." But God has revealed them to us through His Spirit. For the Spirit searches all things, yes, the deep things of God.*
> 1 CORINTHIANS 2:9-10 NKJV

He gives us spiritual gifts and directs us in their use.

> *A spiritual gift is given to each of us so we can help each other. To one person the Spirit gives the ability to give wise advice; to another the same Spirit gives a message of special knowledge. The same Spirit gives great faith to another, and to someone else the one Spirit gives the gift of healing. He gives one person the power to perform miracles, and another the ability to prophesy. He gives someone else the ability to discern whether a message is from the Spirit of God or from another spirit. Still another person is given the ability to speak in unknown languages, while another is given the ability to interpret what is being said. It is the one and only Spirit who distributes all these gifts. He alone decides which gift each person should have.* 1 CORINTHIANS 12:7-11 NLT

He brings the love of God to fill our empty hearts.

> *And this hope will not lead to disappointment. For we know how dearly God loves us, because He has given us the Holy Spirit to fill our hearts with His love.* ROMANS 5:5 NLT

He sets us apart as God's vessels.

> *That I might be a minister of Jesus Christ to the Gentiles, ministering the gospel of God, that the offering of the Gentiles might be acceptable, sanctified by the Holy Spirit.* ROMANS 15:16 NKJV

He produces His fruit in our lives.

> *But the fruit of the Spirit is love, joy, peace, longsuffering, kindness, goodness, faithfulness, gentleness, self-control. Against such there is no law.* GALATIANS 5:22-23 NKJV

The fruit of the Spirit is not our fruit. It doesn't come from us, but from the Holy Spirit. We don't produce it, own it, or perfect it. The fruit of the Spirit is not something we "work on," it is something we surrender our lives to—we surrender to the love, the joy, the peace, the patience, the kindness, the goodness, the faithfulness, the gentleness and the self-control of the Holy Spirit.

How good, and wise, and wonderful is the work of the Holy Spirit. Without Him coming to us, our lives would be void of everything that really matters.

The Holy Spirit at Work in Us

My Prayer

Thank You, **Jesus** for sending the **Holy Spirit**.

Thank You, **Holy Spirit** for coming to me.

I know that You are working in me just as You have worked in the lives of all who follow **Jesus Christ**. Continue to work in me all that is right, good, fruitful, and beneficial. Fill my heart with Your love, fill my mind with Your thoughts, guide my feet in Your ways, and empower me to serve **Jesus** more faithfully in my life.

Amen.

*If we live by the [Holy] Spirit,
let us also walk by the Spirit.
[If by the Holy Spirit we have our life in God,
let us go forward walking in line,
our conduct controlled by the Spirit.]*

GALATIANS 5:25 AMP

CHAPTER 5

WALKING IN THE SPIRIT

One of the things God asks us to do as His children is to walk. Our walk in the Spirit does not begin with our feet, it begins in our hearts. Joni Erickson Tada, who became a quadriplegic after a serious spinal cord injury, once said, "You can be in a wheelchair and still walk with God."

What does it mean to walk in the Spirit?

WALKING IN THE SPIRIT MEANS the manner in which we live our lives as we grow in our relationship with the Holy Spirit and allow Him to conform us to the image of Jesus Christ. It means a life of trust, of yielding, and of obedience to the Holy Spirit's leading. We cannot be passive, indifferent, or unresponsive to the Holy Spirit if we desire to walk with Him.

> *So now we serve...[under obedience to the promptings] of the Spirit in newness [of life].* ROMANS 7:6 AMP

WALKING IN THE SPIRIT MEANS not trying to make things happen, striving, or being impatient. A farmer knows that he cannot force fruit to grow, nor be anxious to pick fruit that is not ready to be harvested. God will complete the work that His Spirit has begun in us.

> *Being confident of this very thing, that He which hath begun a good work in you will perform it until the day of Jesus Christ.* PHILIPPIANS 1:6 KJV

WALKING IN THE SPIRIT MEANS going at His pace, at a stride that allows us to keep in step with Him. His pace will always keep us in peace. To walk in the Spirit means that we are not trying to get ahead of Him because we think He is moving too slowly to meet our timetable.

The Holy Spirit is not behind us, pushing; He is not ahead of us, running at top speed. He goes at the perfect *pace* to lead us into His perfect *place*. He is not taking us on a sprint, but on a walk, one step at a time, one day at a time.

> *Let me hear of Your unfailing love each morning, for I am trusting You. Show me where to walk, for I give myself to You.* PSALM 143:8 NLT

WALKING IN THE SPIRIT MEANS following His direction and not blazing our own trails; allowing Him to be in all the stops and all the starts; all the quiet places, resting places, and places of renewal and refreshment along the way; all the yeses and all the noes; all the climbing and all the descending; all the going outs and all the coming ins; all the times of labor and all the times of stillness.

> *My times are in Your hands.* PSALM 31:15 AMP

WALKING IN THE SPIRIT MEANS traveling on the Highway of Holiness—taking up our cross; denying ourselves and placing no confidence in the flesh; departing from evil; forsaking sin. To walk in the Spirit is the pure way, the righteous way, and the only way that will glorify God. The *Holy* Spirit will never lead us to walk in an *unholy* way.

> *A highway shall be there, and a road, and it shall be called the Highway of Holiness.* ISAIAH 35:8 NKJV

WALKING IN THE SPIRIT MEANS going in the right direction and arriving at the right destination—the Holy Spirit never gets sidetracked, strays off course, or gives wrong directions. When we walk in the Spirit, we don't need to be anxious about how things will turn out or where things will finish up.

> *Therefore be patient, brethren, until the coming of the Lord. See how the farmer waits for the precious fruit of the earth, waiting patiently for it until it receives the early and latter rain.* JAMES 5:7 NKJV

WALKING IN THE SPIRIT MEANS to walk by faith, confident that the way of the Spirit will always lead us down the center of God's will and straight to His heart.

> *Teach me Your way, O Lord, that I may walk and live in Your truth; direct and unite my heart [solely, reverently] to fear and honor Your name.* PSALM 86:11 AMP

WALKING IN THE SPIRIT MEANS experiencing a life of freedom and fruitfulness. The Spirit frees us from the slave market of sin, from the weight of guilt, from the cloud of condemnation, from the fear of judgment, and from the terrors of the wrath to come. The Spirit brings us into the joys that take us higher than our spirits have ever soared, into the peace that is beyond what our souls can understand, and into the fruits of love that go deeper than our hearts have ever journeyed.

> *Now the Lord is the Spirit; and where the Spirit of the Lord is, there is liberty.* 2 CORINTHIANS 3:17 NKJV

> *But the Holy Spirit produces this kind of fruit in our lives: love, joy, peace, patience, kindness, goodness, faithfulness, gentleness, and self-control.* GALATIANS 5:22-23 NLT

WALKING IN THE SPIRIT MEANS following the Spirit.

The Holy Spirit wants us to follow Him in our choices, in our attitudes, in our thoughts, in our work, in our homes, and in our relationships.

The Holy Spirit wants us to follow Him in our prayers, our worship, our fellowship, and our witness.

The Holy Spirit wants us to follow Him into the light of Jesus, into the knowledge of His will, into the revelation of the Scriptures, into His witness to the world, and into our ministry within the body of Christ.

He walks with us as a guide and a companion. He brings with Him all the supplies we will need for each day's travel. If we have to look back to find Him, it means we are walking too fast. No shortcuts are needed to get us there on time. He wants us to stop when He stops, turn where He turns, and delight in all things He is revealing to us along the way.

> *When the Spirit of truth comes, He will guide you into all truth.* JOHN 16:13 NLT

WALKING IN THE SPIRIT MEANS that we need to turn our full attention to what He is saying, where He is going, and what He is doing in our lives. Turning towards the Holy Spirit means that we will be turning our attention away from the things that distract us and mislead us. As Jesus said, *"We cannot serve two masters."*

We walk by faith when we turn away from the unbelief that displeases the Lord.

> *For we walk by faith, not by sight.* 2 CORINTHIANS 5:7 NKJV

We walk in love when we turn away from a self-centered heart that quenches the Spirit's work.

> *And walk in love, as Christ also hath loved us, and hath given Himself for us an offering and a sacrifice to God for a sweet smelling savor.* EPHESIANS 5:2 KJV

We walk in the light when we turn away from the darkness of going our own way.

> *If we say that we have fellowship with Him, and walk in darkness, we lie, and do not the truth: But if we walk in the light, as He is in the light, we have fellowship one with another, and the blood of Jesus Christ His Son cleanseth us from all sin.* 1 JOHN 1:6-7 KJV

We walk as Jesus walked when we turn away from seeking the approval of others above the approval of God.

> *He who says he abides in Him ought himself also to walk just as He walked.* 1 JOHN 2:6 NKJV

We walk in truth when we turn away from all thinking that is against the mind of Christ.

> *I have no greater joy than to hear that my children walk in truth.* 3 JOHN 1:4 NKJV

We walk in a worthy manner when we turn away from the things that promote our own image.

> *That you would walk worthy of God who calls you into His own kingdom and glory.* 1 THESSALONIANS 2:12 NKJV

We walk wisely when we turn away from foolish talk, thinking and behavior.

> *Walk in wisdom toward them that are without, redeeming the time.* COLOSSIANS 4:5 KJV

We walk properly when we turn away from the things that grieve the Spirit.

> *Let us walk properly as in the day, not in revelry and drunkenness, not in lewdness and lust, not in strife and envy.* ROMANS 13:13 NKJV

We walk in newness of life when we turn away from the old way of living before we knew Christ.

> *Therefore we were buried with Him through baptism into death, that just as Christ was raised from the dead by the glory of the Father, even so we also should walk in newness of life.* ROMANS 6:4 NKJV

As we walk in the Spirit daily, we will find Him taking us from childhood to adulthood, from infancy to maturity, from drinking milk to eating meat, from buds to fruitfulness, from wading places to deep pools, from gladness of heart to fullness of joy. He will take us there along:

> The narrow way. [Matthew 7:14]
>
> The known way. [Psalm 1:6]

The sure way. [Psalm 18:30]

The prepared way. [Psalm 37:23]

The taught way. [Psalm 32:8]

The guided way. [Psalm 25:8-9]

The wise way. [Proverbs 4:11]

The celebrated way. [Psalm 119:14]

The peaceful way. [Luke 1:79]

The Jesus way. [John 14:6]

The Highway of Holiness. [Isaiah 35:8]

The pathway of His footsteps. [Psalm 85:13]

The path of the just. [Proverbs 4:18]

The path that's straight. [Proverbs 4:11]

The path of truth. [Psalm 119:35]

The path of light. [Psalm 119:105]

The path of life. [Psalms 16:11]

The path that's good. [Proverbs 2:9]

The path of preservation. [Proverbs 2:8]

The path through apparent impossibilities. [Isaiah 43:16]

No matter the way, no matter the path, we can be fully assured that when we walk in the Holy Spirit, live in the Holy Spirit, and follow the lead of the Holy Spirit, we will *ALWAYS* be pleasing our Heavenly Father, obeying His word, and glorifying His Son.

My Prayer

Holy Spirit, be my Teacher as I walk with You. If I am to know truth, it must come through Your revelation. If I am to have understanding, it must be heard through Your voice. If I am to have clarity, it must be seen through Your light. If I am to have wisdom, it must be known through Your instruction. If I am to experience change, it must come through Your power. I trust in You today. Please lead me in the paths that are right and good.

Amen.

Notes

¹⁶*But I say, walk by the Spirit,
and you will not carry out the desire of the flesh.*

¹⁷*For the flesh sets its desire against the Spirit,
and the Spirit against the flesh...*

GALATIANS 5:16-17 NASB

CHAPTER 6

THE SPIRIT AGAINST THE FLESH

The way the Holy Spirit wants us to walk is very different from the way we naturally want to walk. The Bible tells us in Galatians 5:16-17 that our flesh (how we live when the Holy Spirit is not in control of our lives) is in direct contrast and conflict with what the Holy Spirit desires for us.

To live in the flesh means that we are living naturally and not supernaturally; it defines the way we would live our lives without the Holy Spirit's presence; it casts us upon our own resources, and separates us from the Spirit's supply.

Consider the flesh and the Spirit having a conversation over different choices we need to make. Here is how it might take place:

The flesh says, "I want to pursue my goals."
The Spirit says, "Pursue My purposes."

The flesh says, "I have great ideas."
The Spirit says, "Seek My wisdom."

The Holy Spirit Book

The flesh says, "I have a great plan."
The Spirit says, "I have a perfect plan."

The flesh says, "I want to draw people through my personality."
The Spirit says, "I want to draw people through My presence."

The flesh says, "Look at my determination."
The Spirit says, "Let Me be in control."

The flesh says, "I have talent."
The Spirit says, "Desire My gifts."

The flesh says, "I am working hard."
The Spirit says, "Receive My power."

The flesh says, "I want to make a difference."
The Spirit says, "I am the Difference Maker."

The flesh says, "I know a lot."
The Spirit says, "I will give you revelation and wisdom after the knowledge of Him.

The flesh says, "I am a clever speaker."
The Spirit says, "I speak the Truth."

The flesh says, "I want to win people over."
The Spirit says, "Walk in My favor."

The flesh says, "I want to keep trying new things to see what will satisfy."
The Spirit says, "Drink of Me and be filled."

The flesh says, "I am a pretty nice person."
The Spirit says, "I am Perfect Love."

The flesh says, "I am doing the best I can."
The Spirit says, "Let Me do it through you."

The Spirit Against the Flesh

The flesh says, "I am weary."
The Spirit says, "I will renew your strength."

The flesh says, "I am trying to live a good life."
The Spirit says, "I will make you holy."

The flesh says, "I need to be dynamic."
The Spirit says, "You need My anointing."

The flesh says, "I want recognition."
The Spirit says, "Seek My approval."

The flesh says, "I want people to like me."
The Spirit says, "I want people to glorify Jesus."

The flesh says, "It's all about me."
The Spirit says, "It's all about Jesus."

The way we have victory in our lives over the demands of the flesh is to walk in the Spirit. We will fail if we try to reason with the flesh or use our own strength to fight it. The way of victory over the flesh is the cross of Jesus Christ. As far as God is concerned, being led or ruled by our flesh is over, and the Holy Spirit has been sent to take over our lives and be in control.

> *Then Jesus said to His disciples, "If anyone desires to come after Me, let him deny himself, and take up his cross, and follow Me. For whoever desires to save his life will lose it, but whoever loses his life for My sake will find it."*
> MATTHEW 16:24-25 NKJV

My Prayer

Lord, have Your way with me.

I want to walk in the **Holy Spirit,**

and walk with the **Holy Spirit**

in surrender, in dependency, in total trust.

I place no confidence in my flesh—

in my own resources, in my own strength,

or in my own understanding.

I lay aside all the things in my life

that are about me and my own way.

I take up my cross to follow You,

I depend upon the **Holy Spirit** to be like You,

I receive from the **Holy Spirit** all I need to live for You,

this day and in all my tomorrows.

Amen.

Notes

*Your ears shall hear a word behind you, saying,
"This is the way, walk in it,"
whenever you turn to the right hand
or whenever you turn to the left.*

ISAIAH 30:21 NKJV

CHAPTER 7

Recognizing the Voice of the Holy Spirit

One day a man was returning home from a long trip overseas. In route, he needed to switch planes for the final leg of his journey. He was weary and couldn't wait to get home to see his family. While waiting in the terminal to make connections, he heard an announcement, "There is a doctor who has just arrived and needs to board this flight. It is an emergency. Our flight is full and we need someone who would be willing to give up their seat."

The man quickly dismissed the idea of giving up his seat. A few moments later he heard the still small voice of the Holy Spirit speak to him, "Give up your seat." The man struggled with what he heard. "But Lord, You know how tired I am, how long I've been gone, and how much I want to be home tonight with my family. There are so many people waiting to get on this flight, could you please ask someone else?"

When he finished speaking, the Lord replied, "I have asked others, but you are the only one who is listening."

When the Holy Spirit speaks, He will speak to us with words and in ways that we will understand. If He wants us to know something, we will know it. If He wants us to go somewhere, He will show us how to get there. If He wants us to do something, He will equip us to do it, in His strength!

Because each member of the Trinity is a divine person, each One has a voice and is a communicator.

God the Father has a voice, and He speaks.

> *The LORD God of heaven, who took me from my father's house and from the land of my family, and who spoke to me and swore to me, saying, "To your descendants I give this land," He will send His angel before you, and you take a wife for my son from there.* GENESIS 24:7 NKJV

Jesus Christ has a voice, and He speaks.

> *The sheep that are My own hear and are listening to My voice; and I know them, and they follow Me.*
> JOHN 10:27 AMP

The Holy Spirit has a voice, and He speaks.

> *Anyone with ears to hear must listen to the Spirit and understand what He is saying to the churches.*
> REVELATION 2:29 NLT

Each person of the Trinity communicates with each other, and They communicate with us.

> *All that belongs to the Father is Mine; this is why I said, "The Spirit will tell you whatever He receives from Me."*
> JOHN 16:15 NLT

Recognizing the Voice of the Holy Spirit

One day, during a Sunday morning service, the minister invited a little boy that he knew to come to the front of the church and stand with his back to the congregation. The minister then pointed to three women in the congregation (one was the child's mother) and asked them to stand at the back of the church facing the child. He then asked each of the women to call out the child's name, Billy, and ask him to turn around. The minister also told Billy to listen carefully to each voice, and to only turn around when he heard the voice of his mother.

The first woman called out to Billy, but he did not respond. The second woman called out to Billy, but he did not respond. When the third woman, who was Billy's mother, called out and asked Billy to turn around, the child turned immediately. The sound of his mother's voice was no mystery to Billy.

The voice of the Lord in our lives is like the sound of no other voice. When we learn to recognize His voice, it will be as familiar as our own mother's voice. Jesus said that when He speaks to His sheep, the sheep recognize His voice and follow Him because they will not follow the voice of a stranger. Because God the Father, the Son, and the Holy Spirit are good communicators, we need to be good listeners.

The Holy Spirit has been sent to us by Jesus to live in us. His Spirit is united with our spirit. Today, when Jesus speaks to us He does not need to speak in an audible voice to be heard or understood. Yes, we have physical ears to hear, but we also have spiritual ears to hear the voice of the Holy Spirit.

The voice of the Holy Spirit in our lives is an inner voice. His voice is closer and more intimate than any audible human voice, for He speaks to us in the deepest part of our beings.

> *The person who is united to the Lord becomes one spirit with Him.* 1 CORINTHIANS 6:17 AMP

> *The Holy One has given you His Spirit, and all of you know the truth.* 1 JOHN 2:20 NLT

We need to be wise and discerning as we listen for God's voice. There are many voices trying to get our attention. The voice of the enemy tries to deceive us to follow his voice, the voice of the world tries to pressure us to follow its demands, and the voice of others tries to persuade us to follow their point of view. Our desire and our prayer should focus on pleasing the Lord in our responses and not hardening our hearts when we hear His voice (Hebrews 3:15). Here are several important truths to help us hear and identify God's voice in our lives:

WHEN THE HOLY SPIRIT SPEAKS TO US, He is clear and specific.

> *Then the Spirit told me to go with them, doubting nothing.* ACTS 11:12 NKJV

WHEN THE HOLY SPIRIT SPEAKS TO US, His voice will most often be a still small voice that is calm and gentle in tone. He will often nudge us or prompt us.

> *And after the earthquake a fire, but the Lord was not in the fire; and after the fire [a sound of gentle stillness and] a still, small voice.* 1 KINGS 19:12 AMP

WHEN THE HOLY SPIRIT SPEAKS TO US, it will be in agreement with Christ's heart, will, and ways, and will be consistent with God's divine nature and character.

> *When He has brought His own sheep outside, He walks on before them, and the sheep follow Him because they know His voice. They will never [on any account] follow a strang-*

er, but will run away from him because they do not know the voice of strangers or recognize their call. JOHN 10:4-5 AMP

WHEN THE HOLY SPIRIT SPEAKS TO US, we will have peace, and we will walk in peace as we obey.

And let the peace that comes from Christ rule in your hearts. For as members of one body you are called to live in peace. And always be thankful. COLOSSIANS 3:15 NLT

I will listen [with expectancy] to what God the Lord will say, for He will speak peace to His people. PSALM 85:8 AMP

WHEN THE HOLY SPIRIT SPEAKS TO US, He will always be in agreement with the Truth of God's Word.

But when He, the Spirit of Truth (the Truth-giving Spirit) comes, He will guide you into all the Truth (the whole, full Truth). JOHN 16:13 AMP

WHEN THE HOLY SPIRIT SPEAKS TO US, we need to be good listeners who desire to obey.

Now Samuel did not yet know the LORD, neither was the word of the LORD yet revealed unto him. And the LORD called Samuel again the third time. And he arose and went to Eli, and said, Here am I; for thou didst call me. And Eli perceived that the LORD had called the child. Therefore Eli said unto Samuel, Go, lie down: and it shall be, if He call thee, that thou shalt say, Speak, LORD; for Thy servant heareth. So Samuel went and lay down in his place. And the LORD came, and stood, and called as at other times, Samuel, Samuel. Then Samuel answered, Speak; for Thy servant heareth. 1 SAMUEL 3:7-10 KJV

Like young Samuel, we need to ask the Lord to speak to us because we want to listen to what He is saying. In time, we will learn to identify His voice more clearly, and that clarity will come to us as we follow and obey.

Remember, God is light, not darkness, and He wants us, as children of the day, to walk in the light of His will. God wants us to know His will more than we want to know His will, and He has many ways of speaking to us and revealing His will. God will speak to us through the Scriptures, through His Son, and through the witness of the Holy Spirit. We also discover in the Scriptures that God can speak to us through circumstances, through dreams and visions, through the voice of His people, through spiritual gifts, or through His angelic messengers.

The question we should be asking is not whether God speaks to us, but whether or not we are good listeners and are willing to do His will from the heart once He has revealed it to us. God looks at our hearts, and the reason *why* we do something is as important as *what* we do.

A wise person once said, "Obedience precedes revelation." Those who are willing to know, will know, and those who know, will know more…their light will grow brighter, their understanding will grow clearer, their footsteps will grow surer, their discernment will grow sharper, their confidence will grow stronger, and their trust will grow deeper.

> *To those who listen to My teaching, more understanding will be given, and they will have an abundance of knowledge. But for those who are not listening, even what little understanding they have will be taken away from them.*
> MATTHEW 13:12 NLT

Recognizing the Voice of the Holy Spirit

Jesus said, "Anyone who wants to do the will of God will know whether My teaching is from God or is merely My own." JOHN 7:17 NLT

The Holy Spirit Book

My Prayer

Lord, help me to know Your voice, to welcome it
and receive it. Like Samuel, I ask You to speak to me,
for I am listening. By Your grace, I not only want to hear
Your voice, but I also want to follow and obey.
I want to do what is pleasing in Your sight.
Thank You for the voice of the **Holy Spirit** in my life.
With my spiritual ears I will listen to Him
as He speaks Truth to me, brings **Jesus'** words to me,
works Your will in me, reveals the Scriptures to me,
convicts me of sin, establishes me in righteousness,
builds me up in my faith, encourages me in my walk,
uses His gifts in me to touch others, and manifests
Your glory through the fruits of love
that He places in my heart.

Amen.

Notes

SECTION III

The POWER of the HOLY SPIRIT

*But you will receive **power**
when the Holy Spirit comes upon you.*

ACTS 1:8 NLT

CHAPTER 8

THE IMPORTANCE OF SPIRITUAL POWER

Years ago, driving a car meant the driver had two distinct choices at the gas station, regular gas or ethyl. To put it simply, if you had a big car with a powerful, high performance engine, you needed ethyl gas. The car could still run on regular gas, but it would not perform well. With ethyl in the tank, the car would sing; without ethyl, the car would ping.

As believers, we are not to fill up our lives at the gas pump of "regular living." We cannot live a Kingdom life on low octane human fuel. Instead, God wants us to fill up our lives at the source of "supernatural living." That source, that Life, is the Holy Spirit.

Because spiritual power *only* comes from a supernatural source, it *cannot* come from a natural or human source. It is not found in personal influence, in personal success, in personal achievements, in personal wealth, nor in personal education. Kingdom work can only be done in a Kingdom way, and the way God does all His work is through the Holy Spirit.

> *This is the word of the LORD to Zerubbabel: "Not by might nor by power, but by My Spirit," says the LORD of hosts.*
> ZECHARIAH 4:6 NKJV

Only the Holy Spirit can make it possible for us to experience the life God has called us to live. In fact, God has not given us the option to "get by" on the regular gasoline of our own resources. God does not tell us to do the best we can (even if we do ping a lot), and He does not tell us to mix fuels. God tells us to *be filled* with the Holy Spirit. We are to draw all our spiritual power from the Holy Spirit alone.

Empowerment by the Holy Spirit is available to every believer. This empowering is essential for holy living and for spiritual service. Jesus spoke about this when He met with His disciples after His resurrection and before He ascended to the right hand of the Father.

> *And being assembled together with them, He commanded them not to depart from Jerusalem, but to wait for the Promise of the Father, "which," He said, "you have heard from Me; for John truly baptized with water, but you shall be baptized with the Holy Spirit not many days from now… you shall receive power when the Holy Spirit has come upon you; and you shall be witnesses to Me in Jerusalem, and in all Judea and Samaria, and to the end of the earth."*
> ACTS 1:4-8 NKJV

Eric Liddell's life was featured in the Academy Award winning movie, *Chariots of Fire*. Eric was a runner and an Olympic champion who later became a missionary to China. In a very poignant scene in the film, Eric spoke these words to a group who had gathered at a running event: "Where does the power come from to see the race to its end? From within." He was speaking of the Holy Spirit.

The Importance of Spiritual Power

Our spiritual journey is for a lifetime, and the needs are great. That is why we have been commanded by God to be filled with the Holy Spirit. Like Eric, every follower of Jesus Christ needs the person, the purpose, and the power of the Holy Spirit within to serve the Lord faithfully and effectively throughout the race until they make it to the finish line. The Holy Spirit has come to make it possible for us to stand and not stumble; to walk and not faint; and to complete the work God has given us to do until the day He calls us home.

> *Therefore, since we are surrounded by such a huge crowd of witnesses to the life of faith, let us strip off every weight that slows us down, especially the sin that so easily trips us up. And let us run with endurance the race God has set before us. We do this by keeping our eyes on Jesus, the champion who initiates and perfects our faith.* HEBREWS 12:1-2 NLT

None of us should push on in our own strength or try running until we are out of gas and end up parked by the side of the road with an empty tank. We not only need to *be filled* with the Spirit, but we also need to *keep on being filled*. His filling is abundant and freely given, and He is more than able to keep us full as we partake of His abundance, moment by moment, and day by day.

My Prayer

Lord, thank You that You have called me

and drawn me to Yourself.

Thank You for saving me and keeping me.

I know You have a purpose for my life

and that I cannot serve You in my own strength.

Thank You for the **Holy Spirit** and for His power.

May I be filled with Him, walk in Him,

live in Him, and find His power within

to run the race You have set before me,

and to run it in a way that pleases You.

Amen.

Notes

*And behold, I will send forth upon you
what My Father has promised;
but remain in the city [Jerusalem]
until you are clothed with **power** from on high.*

LUKE 24:49 AMP

CHAPTER 9

THE MEANING OF SPIRITUAL POWER

There are two important Greek words that are used in Scripture to help us understand the meaning of spiritual power. One word used for power is found in Matthew 10:1. It is the word *exousia*.

> And when He had called unto Him His twelve disciples, He gave them power (exousia) against unclean spirits, to cast them out, and to heal all manner of sickness and all manner of disease. MATTHEW 10:1 KJV

Exousia means having the power of authority. A policeman who is able to stop moving traffic on a busy street is an example of the power of authority. The policeman does not have the physical strength to stop the traffic, but because he represents the law of the land, and because he is backed by the police force, he can direct the traffic to stop or to go.

The other Greek word that is used for power is *dunamis*. In English, this word can be translated as *dynamo* or *dynamite*. This word is found in Acts 1:8.

> *But ye shall receive power (dunamis), after that the Holy Ghost is come upon you: and ye shall be witnesses unto Me both in Jerusalem, and in all Judaea, and in Samaria, and unto the uttermost part of the earth.* ACTS 1:8 KJV

In this passage Jesus was not speaking about the power of authority, but the power of might, strength, enabling, equipping, and boldness that would be upon and within the lives of those gathered in The Upper Room on the day of Pentecost. Receiving the Spirit's power would bring a dynamic change into each life.

Jesus did not say that receiving the *dunamis* power of the Holy Spirit was optional. He said that it was essential for them to be His witnesses. Their witness to the world was to be more than a witness of His life on Earth and His death on the cross; it was also to bring witness to His resurrection, His ascension, and His glorification at the right hand of the Father. Their lives were also a witness to the promised gift of the Holy Spirit that would equip them for service. It was through their witness that the living Jesus was proclaimed and demonstrated in both word and power.

> *Once when He was eating with them, He commanded them, "Do not leave Jerusalem until the Father sends you the gift He promised, as I told you before."* ACTS 1:4 NLT

> *The apostles testified powerfully to the resurrection of the Lord Jesus, and God's great blessing was upon them all.* ACTS 4:33 NLT

The apostle Peter is a good example of the difference the power of the Holy Spirit can make in a believer's life.

> *Now when they saw the boldness of Peter and John, and per-*

> *ceived that they were uneducated and untrained men, they marveled. And they realized that they had been with Jesus.*
> ACTS 4:13 NKJV

Peter was often full of self-confidence, and boasted of his natural strength and determination. He even vowed he would never deny the Lord. Yet, when Jesus was betrayed, Peter became a cowering, fearful, weak person who denied the Lord three times. However, after the day of Pentecost, when the Holy Spirit had come upon Peter and filled him with *dunamis* power, Peter was able to stand in front of thousands of Jews in Jerusalem and proclaim with *great boldness* the Gospel of Jesus Christ. It was in this sermon that Peter declared where this power had come from:

> *This Jesus God has raised up, of which we are all witnesses. Therefore being exalted to the right hand of God, and having received from the Father the promise of the Holy Spirit, He poured out this which you now see and hear.*
> ACTS 2:32-33 NKJV

Besides empowering the believer for Kingdom service, there are other significant reasons why the Holy Spirit needs to come upon every believer in power and fill them. The following Scriptures help us understand the importance of *dunamis* power in our daily lives and how defeated and ineffective we would be without it.

SPIRITUAL POWER IS NEEDED to deal effectively with the demonic world.

> *Then they were all amazed and spoke among themselves, saying, "What a word this is! For with authority and **power** He commands the unclean spirits, and they come out."*
> LUKE 4:36 NKJV

Spiritual power is needed for God to use us to do mighty things that will touch others.

> *And Stephen, full of faith and **power**, did great wonders and signs among the people.* ACTS 6:8 NKJV

Spiritual power is needed to fill our lives with joy, peace, and hope.

> *Now may the God of hope fill you with all joy and peace in believing, that you may abound in hope by **the power of the Holy Spirit**.* ROMANS 15:13 NKJV

Spiritual power is needed to effectively preach the Word of God.

> *And my speech and my preaching were not with persuasive words of human wisdom, but in demonstration **of the Spirit and of power**.* 1 CORINTHIANS 2:4 NKJV

Spiritual power is needed to be strong in the Lord.

> *And He said to me, "My grace is sufficient for you, for My strength is made perfect in weakness." Therefore most gladly I will rather boast in my infirmities, that **the power of Christ** may rest upon me.* 2 CORINTHIANS 12:9 NKJV

Spiritual power is needed to walk in all that God has for us.

> *Now to Him who is able to do exceedingly abundantly above all that we ask or think, **according to the power** that works in us.* EPHESIANS 3:20 NKJV

Spiritual power is needed to live a holy life.

> *That you may walk worthy of the Lord, fully pleasing Him, being fruitful in every good work and increasing in the*

The Meaning of Spiritual Power

*knowledge of God; strengthened with all might, **according to His glorious power**, for all patience and longsuffering with joy.* COLOSSIANS 1:10-11 NKJV

The life we have been called to live as believers and followers of Jesus Christ is not a shallow life, but an abundant life; not a pitiful life, but a plentiful life; not an ordinary life, but a supernatural life. This life is available to all believers through the person, the purpose and the power of the Holy Spirit.

My Prayer

Lord Jesus, what a wonderful **Savior** You are. Thank You for coming and giving Your life for me so I might be saved; for Your resurrection and for giving me hope and a future; for Your ascension and sending the **Holy Spirit** to equip and empower me to be Your witness. Help me be Your faithful witness who is true to Your Word. Thank You for making this possible through the power of Your **Holy Spirit**.

Amen.

Notes

¹⁶*So He came to Nazareth,
where He had been brought up. And as His custom was,
He went into the synagogue on the Sabbath day,
and stood up to read.*

¹⁷*And He was handed the book of the prophet Isaiah.
And when He had opened the book,
He found the place where it was written:*

¹⁸*"The Spirit of the LORD is upon Me,
because He has anointed Me
to preach the gospel to the poor;
He has sent Me to heal the brokenhearted,
to proclaim liberty to the captives
and recovery of sight to the blind,
to set at liberty those who are oppressed;*

¹⁹*to proclaim the acceptable year of the LORD."*

LUKE 4:16-19 NKJV

CHAPTER 10

THE RESULTS
OF SPIRITUAL POWER

*I*n the passage on the adjacent page, Jesus read from the Scriptures concerning the coming Messiah. When He was finished, Jesus sat down and declared that He was the fulfillment of the truth Isaiah had written. As the Messiah, Jesus was also proclaiming that because the Holy Spirit had anointed Him, He had the power to preach the Gospel, bring healing, give liberty, recover sight, and release the oppressed. It was the truth of who Jesus was and the power that He had through the Holy Spirit that led to the supernatural experiences He brought to those in need.

It is the truth of God that will lead us into the experiences God has for us. The *truth* of the Gospel is that Jesus came and died for our sins so that we could be forgiven, justified, and made right with God. It is because of this truth that we can *experience* the Gospel when Christ enters into our hearts and we are born again through the Holy Spirit's presence.

Another way we can see how truth and experience work together is by looking at the example of a house. In order for a house to be built and to stand, it needs to be anchored to a good foundation. Truth is likened to the foundation that a house is built upon. Our foundation is Christ and His Word. We also understand that a house is not built upon a solid foundation so that it can be admired and studied; a house is built to be lived in. People are meant to *experience* a house by living in it. Even so, as believers, we not only build our lives upon Christ, but we also experience His life day by day through living in the Holy Spirit.

> *If we live in the Spirit, let us also walk in the Spirit.*
> GALATIANS 5:25 NKJV

Consider how the truth of the Holy Spirit's power was experienced by others.

The Power of the Holy Spirit in the Life of Jesus

> *Then John testified, "I saw the Holy Spirit descending like a dove from heaven and resting upon Him."* JOHN 1:32 NLT

According to Jewish law, the public ministry of the priests in the tabernacle was to begin at the age of thirty.

> *From thirty years old and up to fifty years old you shall number them, all who enter for service to do the work in the Tent of Meeting.* NUMBERS 4:23 AMP

When Jesus came up out of the waters of baptism, He was 30 years of age. It was at this time that the Holy Spirit came upon Jesus and anointed Him with power to begin His public ministry.

The Results of Spiritual Power

> *God anointed Jesus of Nazareth with the Holy Spirit and with power, who went about doing good and healing all who were oppressed by the devil, for God was with Him.*
> ACTS 10:38 NKJV

Jesus Himself knew He needed the anointing power of the Holy Spirit to do the work God called Him to do. Although Jesus was fully God and fully man, He did not do His mighty works as the Son of God, but as the Son of Man who was anointed and empowered by the Holy Spirit.

Jesus wants to send us in the same way that He was sent (John 20:21). Because Jesus was sent by His Father, with the power of the Holy Spirit upon Him, how much more, then, do we need the Holy Spirit's power to do what God has called us to do?

> *Most assuredly, I say to you, he who believes in Me, the works that I do he will do also; and greater works than these he will do, because I go to My Father.* JOHN 14:12 NKJV

The Power of the Holy Spirit in the Lives of Others

Throughout history, men and women of God have testified to the empowering ministry of the Holy Spirit upon their lives. A collection of some of these accounts can be found in the book *Deeper Experiences of Famous Christians* by J. Gilchrist Lawson. Some of the stories told in this book belong to great men of faith like Fénelon, John Bunyan, John Wesley, Charles G. Finney, George Müller, General Booth, and D.L. Moody.

In the account in this book given by Moody we read:

> "Moody continued to hunger for a deepening of his own spiritual life and experience. He had been greatly used of God, but felt that there were much greater things in store for him. The year 1871 was a critical one with him. He realized more and more how little he was fitted by personal acquirements for his work, and how much he needed to be qualified for service by the Holy Spirit's power. This realization was deepened by conversations he had with two ladies who sat on the front pew in his church. He could see by the expression of their faces that they were praying.
>
> At the close of the service they would say to him, "We have been praying for you." "Why don't you pray for the people?" Mr. Moody would ask. "Because you need the power of the Spirit," was the reply. "I need the power! Why," said he, in relating the incident afterwards, "I thought I had power. I had the largest congregation in Chicago, and there were many conversions. I was in a sense satisfied. But right along those two Godly women kept praying for me, and their earnest talk about the anointing for special service set me thinking. Soon I came to a point where I didn't want to live if I could not have this power for service."

Later on in this account we read:

> "Mr. Moody went east to New York City to collect funds for the sufferers from the Chicago fire, but his heart and soul were crying out for the power from on high. "My heart was not in the work of begging," says he. "I could not appeal. I was crying all the time that God would fill me with His Spirit. Well, one day, in the city of New York—oh, what a day! —I cannot describe it, I seldom refer to it; it is almost too sacred an experience to name. Paul had an experience of which he never spoke for fourteen years. I can

only say that God revealed Himself to me, and I had such an experience of His love that I had to ask Him to stay His hand. I went to preaching again. The sermons were not different; I did not present any new truths; and yet hundreds were converted. I would not now be placed back where I was before that blessed experience if you should give me all the world— it would be as the small dust of the balance."

In his own book on spiritual power, Moody makes this statement regarding the importance of receiving the Holy Spirit's power:

"We read in John 20:22: And when He had said this, He breathed on them, and said to them, "Receive the Holy Spirit." Then see Luke 24:49: "Behold, I send the Promise of My Father upon you; but tarry in the city of Jerusalem until you are endued with power from on high." The first passage tells us He had raised those pierced and wounded hands over them and breathed upon them and said, "Receive the Holy Spirit." And I haven't a doubt they received Him then, but not in such mighty power as afterward when qualified for their work. It was not in fullness that He gave Him to them then, but if they had been like a good many now, they would have said, "I have enough now; I am not going to tarry; I am going to work." (Taken from the book *Spiritual Power* by D.L. Moody. See also *Why God Used D.L. Moody* by R.A. Torrey.)

Below are some thoughts from other well-known servants of the Lord about the power of the Holy Spirit.

JONATHAN GOFORTH (1859-1936)—*a Presbyterian missionary to China*

> "My conviction is that the divine power, so manifest in the church at Pentecost, was nothing more nor less than what we should expect in the church today! God never builds His temple by might or by power, but always by His Spirit. I believe the Scriptures clearly mean that the Lord Jesus planned that the Holy Spirit should continue among us with as mighty manifestation as at Pentecost."

CHARLES FINNEY (1792-1875)—*teacher, lawyer, evangelist, pastor, professor of theology and college president. Used by God to bring great revival to America.*

> "Every Christian possesses a measure of the Spirit of Christ already. In conversion to Christ, the soul has to relate directly and personally to Christ. In the baptism of the Holy Spirit there is an enduement of power for ministry. The baptism poured out upon the disciples on the day of Pentecost was an indispensable qualification for success in their ministry. But the baptism itself was a divine purifying, an anointing bestowing on them a divine illumination. It filled them with faith and love, with peace and power, so their words were made sharp in the hearts of God's enemies, quick and powerful."

OSWALD CHAMBERS (1874-1917)—*author, teacher, chaplin*

> "After His resurrection, Jesus breathed on the disciples and said, 'Receive ye the Holy Spirit.' At that time He imparted the Holy Spirit to them and quickened them. Then on the day of Pentecost the disciples were baptized by the

personal Holy Spirit—the quickening became an equipping. The baptism of the Holy Spirit is the complete uniting of the quickened believer with Christ Himself."

There are a multitude of stories and testimonies that share the change that came into their lives, and the power that came into the ministries of God's people through the years. The same Holy Spirit that empowered and equipped them is also available to us today. Through the years, God hasn't changed, Jesus hasn't changed, and the Holy Spirit hasn't changed. What He has done before He will do again, and will continue to do until the return of Jesus Christ.

> *For the promise is to you and to your children,* ***and to all*** *who are afar off, as many as the Lord our God will call.*
> ACTS 2:39 NKJV

My Prayer

Jesus, what a perfect work You have done,

what a perfect **Savior** You are, and thank You

for sending the perfect Helper, the **Holy Spirit**.

Thank You that the **Holy Spirit** has come,

not only to be with me and to live in me,

but also to fill me and empower me to serve You.

I know that without the **Holy Spirit's** presence

and power You could not have pleased the **Father**,

done His will, and completed the work

He sent You to do. Help me to realize

how dependent I am on the **Holy Spirit**

day by day, and moment by moment,

and help me to do His will today and every day.

Amen.

Notes

SECTION IV

The PROMISE of the HOLY SPIRIT

[38] Peter replied,
"Each of you must repent of your sins
and turn to God, and be baptized
in the name of Jesus Christ
for the forgiveness of your sins.
Then you will receive
the gift of the Holy Spirit.

[39] **This promise** is to you,
to your children,
and to those far away—
all who have been called
by the Lord our God."

ACTS 2:38-39 NLT

CHAPTER 11

THE PROMISE FOR ALL BELIEVERS

God makes promises for the purpose of fulfilling them. He can fulfill His promises because every promise is in agreement with His will, and because He has the power to fulfill each one He has made.

His promises and His gifts come to us through grace, and we receive His promises and His gifts through faith. His gifts are grace gifts, which means they are freely given. Every promise of God is a grace promise, and every gift of God is a grace gift.

Two of God's greatest gifts include the gift of salvation and the gift of the Holy Spirit. John spoke of these two gifts coming to us through the life and ministry of Jesus Christ. John spoke of the gift of salvation when He said, "*Look! The Lamb of God who takes away the sin of the world!*" John 1:29 NLT. In this passage the gift of salvation is referred to as "(Jesus) the Lamb of God taking away the sin of the world."

John also spoke of the gift of the Holy Spirit when He said, "*The one on whom you see the Spirit descend and rest is the one who will* **baptize with the Holy Spirit**," John 1:33 NLT. In this passage the gift of the Holy Spirit is referred to as "(Jesus) baptizing with the Holy Spirit."

Today, the gift of salvation is available to all. Even though this is true, it does not mean that everyone *automatically* has the gift of salvation. The gift of salvation is received and appropriated by an individual through personal faith.

It is also true that the gift of the Holy Spirit (the baptism with the Holy Spirit) is available to every believer in Jesus Christ. Even though this is true, it does not mean that everyone who believes in Jesus Christ *automatically* has the gift of the baptism with the Holy Spirit. This gift is also received and appropriated by an individual believer through personal faith.

The Scriptures tell us that both Jesus and the Holy Spirit participate in these two grace gifts. It is Jesus' death upon the cross that makes the gift of our salvation possible, and it is the resurrected and ascended Jesus that makes the gift of the baptism with the Holy Spirit possible.

When we believe in Jesus' atonement and receive Him as our Savior by faith, it is the Holy Spirit who enters within us, and we are born again. When the ascended Jesus baptizes us with the Holy Spirit by faith, it is the Holy Spirit who comes upon us, fills us, and empowers us.

There is a great difference between being born again and being baptized with the Holy Spirit. When we are born again, the Holy Spirit becomes resident within our spirits. Everyone who has believed in Jesus and received Him by faith has the Holy Spirit living within them.

> *If anyone does not possess the [Holy] Spirit of Christ, he is none of His [he does not belong to Christ, is not truly a child of God].* ROMANS 8:9 AMP

When Jesus baptizes and fills us with the Holy Spirit, the Holy Spirit is not only *resident* within us, but He also becomes *president* within us...a Spirit-filled life is a life lived under the power and control of the Holy Spirit.

The Holy Spirit is God's promise for all believers.

The *promise of the presence* of the Holy Spirit is fulfilled when we receive our salvation by faith. The *promise of the power* of the Holy Spirit is fulfilled when we receive the baptism with the Holy Spirit by faith.

When we are born again we receive a complete Holy Spirit and not a partial Holy Spirit. However, we do not receive the *power* of the Holy Spirit until Jesus baptizes us with the Holy Spirit... this is Jesus' gift to us that was promised by His Father.

> *This Jesus God has raised up, of which we are all witnesses. Therefore being exalted to the right hand of God, and having received from the Father* **the promise** *of the Holy Spirit, He poured out this which you now see and hear.*
> ACTS 2:32-33 NKJV

Another way we can see the distinction between the gift of Holy Spirit's *presence* in our lives and His *power* upon our lives is found in the following passage of Scripture:

> *Then Jesus said to them again, "Peace to you! [Just] as the Father has sent Me forth, so I am sending you." And having said this, He breathed on them and said to them, "Receive the Holy Spirit!"* JOHN 20:21-22 AMP

In the above passage, Jesus breathed on them and they received within them the presence of the Holy Spirit. However, even though the Holy Spirit was now within them, Jesus further commanded them to wait in Jerusalem until He would baptize them with the Holy Spirit's power.

> *And behold, I will send forth upon you what My Father has **promised**; but remain in the city [Jerusalem] until you are clothed with power from on high.* LUKE 24:49 AMP

Throughout history, many respected Christian leaders have written about the Holy Spirit and recognized the difference between the promise of His presence and the promise of His power.

R.A. TORREY (1856-1928)—*American evangelist, pastor, educator, and author.*

> "The promise of the Father means the baptism with the Holy Spirit (see Acts 2:39)." (Taken from the book, *The Person and Work of the Holy Spirit*, by R.A. Torrey.)

MARTIN LLOYD JONES (1899-1981)—*Welsh Protestant minister, preacher and medical doctor. Influential in the British evangelical movement.*

> "These men are not only believers, they are regenerate men, the Holy Spirit has been breathed upon them, yet they have not been baptized with the Holy Spirit." (Taken from the book, *The Baptism and Gifts of the Holy Spirit*, by Martin Lloyd Jones.)

The promise of the Holy Spirit being poured out was spoken by God through the prophets. Here is the promise spoken through the prophets Isaiah and Joel:

The Promise for All Believers

> *For I will pour water on him who is thirsty, and floods on the dry ground; I will pour My Spirit **on** your descendants, and My blessing **on** your offspring.* ISAIAH 44:3 NKJV

> *I will pour out My Spirit **upon** all people. Your sons and daughters will prophesy. Your old men will dream dreams, and your young men will see visions. In those days I will pour out My Spirit even on servants—men and women alike.* JOEL 2:28-29 NLT

It is important to know that these promises were not given to one specific group of people, or one specific type of ministry, but for all those who believe.

And this is the promise Jesus made to His disciples just before He ascended to heaven:

> *But you shall receive power when the Holy Spirit has come **upon** you; and you shall be witnesses to Me in Jerusalem, and in all Judea and Samaria, and to the end of the earth.* ACTS 1:8 NKJV

At this time Jesus' work, including His death on the cross, was finished. In the future and until His return, His work would be continued, in an even greater way, through His people, throughout the world.

> *I tell you the truth, anyone who believes in Me will do the same works I have done, and even greater works, because I am going to be with the Father.* JOHN 14:12 NLT

Even though it was Jesus' will to send His people forth to do His work, He knew they were not equipped to go. Only He could make that possible by sending the Holy Spirit to empower them. His instruction to them was to wait for the Holy

Spirit to come upon them before they went out to be His witnesses. His instruction is the same to us today.

His promise was not limited to a certain group at a certain time, and then would go away. The gift of the baptism with the Holy Spirit was not just for the apostles or the early believers mentioned in the book of Acts. His promise was for each believer, in every generation, until His return. Our need of Him today, His fullness and His power is just as great, or even greater, than it was 2000 years ago.

> *For the promise is to you and to your children, and to all who are afar off, as many as the Lord our God will call.*
> ACTS 2:39 NKJV

The Promise for All Believers

My Prayer

Lord, thank You for keeping Your promises.

Thank You for every good and perfect gift

that comes from You.

Thank You for Your grace, upon grace, upon grace.

Thank You for giving freely, abundantly,

and for giving the very best gifts.

Thank You for the gift of so great a salvation,

and thank You for the gift of the Holy Spirit.

I want to receive all that You have for me

and all that You have provided for me

through Your Son, and through the Holy Spirit.

Amen.

*The Spirit of the LORD will rest on Him,
the Spirit of wisdom and understanding,
the Spirit of counsel and strength,
the Spirit of knowledge and the fear of the LORD.*

ISAIAH 11:2 NLT

CHAPTER 12

ONE HOLY SPIRIT, MANY MINISTRIES

The Holy Spirit had many ministries in the life of Jesus. Jesus was *conceived* by the Holy Spirit. He was *indwelt* by the Holy Spirit His entire life, and at the Jordan River, Jesus was *anointed* with the Holy Spirit when the Spirit descended upon Him. It was this particular ministry of the Holy Spirit that would equip Jesus for the next three plus years of completing the work God called Him to do. If Jesus himself—the Son of God—needed to be anointed by the Holy Spirit to do His Father's will, then how much more do we need the same anointing power?

> *God anointed Jesus of Nazareth with the Holy Spirit and with power, who went about doing good and healing all who were oppressed by the devil, for God was with Him.*
> ACTS 10:38 NKJV

Jesus told us of three distinct ways that the Holy Spirit would minister in the lives of believers.

1. Jesus told us that the Holy Spirit would be **with us**. This is His promise of spiritual companionship.

> *The Spirit of truth, whom the world cannot receive, because it neither sees Him nor knows Him; but you know Him, for He dwells **with you** and will be in you.* JOHN 14:17 NKJV

Jesus is now in heaven, at the right hand of the Father. Before He left Earth and ascended to His Father, He assured us that He would not leave us alone. Jesus told us that the Holy Spirit would always be with us, even after He left. Today, it is the Holy Spirit's presence we enjoy. He is with us through every circumstance, every step, every trial, every difficulty, and every heartbeat of life. He doesn't come and go, or visit us on various occasions, but He is with us always. *He is the Holy Spirit, our constant companion.*

2. Jesus told us the Holy Spirit would be *in us*. This is His promise of spiritual intimacy.

> *The Spirit of truth, whom the world cannot receive, because it neither sees Him nor knows Him; but you know Him, for He dwells with you and will be **in you**.* JOHN 14:17 NKJV

The Holy Spirit's presence is not only *with you*, but greater still, the Holy Spirit is present *in you*. The Holy Spirit entered your life when you received Jesus Christ as your Lord and Savior. This experience is called the "new birth" or being "born again" of the Spirit (John 3).

The promise of the Holy Spirit being in us and changing us from within was spoken of by God through the prophets. Here is the promise spoken through the prophet Ezekiel:

> *I will give you a new heart and put a new spirit within you; I will take the heart of stone out of your flesh and give you a heart of flesh. I will put My Spirit within you and cause you*

to walk in My statutes, and you will keep My judgments and do them. EZEKIEL 36:26-27 NKJV

Through the new birth, the Holy Spirit joins Himself to our spirit and we become united with Him. When the Holy Spirit comes to live in us, it means God's light, truth, life and love have come. This means that the Holy Spirit is closer, nearer, and dearer to you than any other person could ever be. *He is the intimate Holy Spirit.*

3. Jesus told us the Holy Spirit would come **upon us**. This is His promise of spiritual power—when we are baptized with the Holy Spirit.

> *You shall receive power when the Holy Spirit has come upon you; and you shall be witnesses to Me in Jerusalem, and in all Judea and Samaria, and to the end of the earth.*
> ACTS 1:8 NKJV

Even though the disciples received the life of the Holy Spirit within them, they still had not received the power of the Holy Spirit upon them. This is why Jesus told them to wait for His promise to be fulfilled before they went into the world as His witnesses. This happened to them on the Feast of Pentecost (Acts 1 and 2). Like the disciples, it is important for us to have both the Scriptural understanding of Jesus' promise as well as the personal experience of receiving the promise of the Holy Spirit upon our lives. *He is the empowering Holy Spirit.*

Although each of us will serve God differently, according to His specific will for our lives, each of us needs to be empowered by the Holy Spirit to serve Him effectively.

> *Jesus said to them again, "Peace to you! As the Father has sent Me, I also send you."* JOHN 20:21 NKJV

The Holy Spirit has come to fulfill all that Jesus has promised. It is Jesus who said He would baptize us with the Holy Spirit. It is God's will that each one of His children be empowered and filled with the Holy Spirit, walk in the Spirit, live in the Spirit, and be led by the Spirit.

One Holy Spirit, Many Ministries

My Prayer

LORD, how needy I am

and how gracious and abundant You are

in Your grace and provision for me.

How thankful I am that I can continue

to have more of You.

Thank You for fulfilling Your promise

of the HOLY SPIRIT and for all the ways

He has come to minister to me and work through me.

I am thankful for His presence and His power,

and that You sent Him to be with me,

to be in me, and to come upon me.

HOLY SPIRIT, I want to receive Your

complete ministry in my life.

AMEN.

And they were all filled with the Holy Spirit.

ACTS 2:4 NKJV

CHAPTER 13

THE FULLNESS OF THE HOLY SPIRIT

*J*esus experienced the power and the filling of the Holy Spirit in His own life and ministry (Luke 4:1). He also promised the power and the filling of the Holy Spirit to His followers. We need both the Scriptural understanding of Jesus' promise as well as the personal experience of receiving the promise of the Holy Spirit.

There are many ways the Scriptures present the fulfillment of Jesus' promise of spiritual power and the fullness of the Holy Spirit. The Bible uses a variety of words and phrases to describe this fulfillment. Two of these phrases are, "the baptism with the Holy Spirit" and "the filling with the Holy Spirit." In Acts 2:4 we read that all the believers who were baptized with the Holy Spirit on the Feast of Pentecost were also filled with the Holy Spirit at the same time. The experience of the baptism and filling with the Holy Spirit is God's will for us. It should not be a mystery to us. It should not be a "guess so" or a "hope so" attitude, but rather, a "know so" reality, just as it was for the first believers.

When Peter spoke to the thousands of Jews who were in Jerusalem for the feast of Pentecost (Shavuot), he was very sure about what had taken place, and acknowledged the sudden transformation in his own life. Peter was not empowered and filled with the Holy Spirit gradually, over a period of months or years, but in a moment when the Holy Spirit was poured out upon him and the others in The Upper Room.

Although each of us may not have the exact same experience that Peter and the other disciples had as recorded in the book of Acts, we can still receive the same Holy Spirit's empowering ministry and fullness today that Peter and the others received back then (Acts 2:39).

Even though everyone's experience of salvation may be different, the important thing is that we know we are saved and born again of the Holy Spirit. Similarly, even though every believer's experience of the baptism with the Holy Spirit may be different, the important thing is that we know with certainty that we have been empowered, filled, and equipped by the Holy Spirit to serve the Lord and do His will.

"You must believe that you can be filled. (If you believe the thinking that you received everything God has for you the day you received Christ as your Savior, you will never move on to the fullness.)" —A.W. Tozer.

The Baptism with the Holy Spirit

The word baptism is used in various ways in Scripture, and there are clear Biblical distinctions between each one. Three of these ways can be identified as the Baptism of **Profession**, the Baptism of **Position**, and the Baptism of **Power**.

The Fullness of the Holy Spirit

The Baptism of Profession
This is the baptism in water, and is an outward profession of the faith of a believer who has repented of sin and inwardly believed in Jesus Christ as their Savior.

> *Peter replied, "Each of you must repent of your sins and turn to God, and **be baptized in the name of Jesus Christ** for the forgiveness of your sins."* ACTS 2:38 NLT

The Baptism of Position
This is the baptism when we are placed positionally into the Body of Christ. This baptism into the Body of Christ is done by the Holy Spirit the moment we receive Christ as our Savior.

> *For as the body is one and has many members, but all the members of that one body, being many, are one body, so also is Christ. **For by one Spirit we were all baptized into one body**—whether Jews or Greeks, whether slaves or free—and have all been made to drink into one Spirit.*
> 1 CORINTHIANS 12:12-13 NKJV

The Baptism of Power
This is the baptism when, as believers, the Holy Spirit comes upon us in power. We receive the baptism of power from Jesus, who is the only one who baptizes with the Holy Spirit.

> *I indeed baptized you with water, but **He (Jesus) will baptize you with the Holy Spirit…but you shall receive power** when the Holy Spirit has come upon you; and you shall be witnesses to Me in Jerusalem, and in all Judea and Samaria, and to the end of the earth.* MARK 1:8 & ACTS 1:8 NKJV

The following charts make it simple to see the Biblical distinctions between each of the three baptisms described on the previous page.

The Baptism of Profession	
Agent	John
Element	in water
Purpose	repentance and profession
Scripture	Acts 2:38

The Baptism of Position	
Agent	the Holy Spirit
Element	into the Body of Christ
Purpose	unity and fellowship
Scripture	I Corinthians 12:12-13

The Baptism of Power	
Agent	Jesus
Element	with the Holy Spirit
Purpose	purity and power
Scripture	Mark 1:8 and Acts 1:8

The agent, element, and purpose for each baptism are described in more detail below. Refer back to the charts as you read.

When we are baptized in water:

John was the original agent of this baptism; he was the one doing the baptizing.

> *Then Jerusalem, all Judea, and all the region around the Jordan went out to him (John) and were **baptized by him (John)** in the Jordan, confessing their sins.*
> MATTHEW 3:5-6 NKJV

All who were baptized by John were baptized in water. Water is the element of this baptism.

> *I indeed **baptize you with water** unto repentance.*
> MATTHEW 3:11 NKJV

The purpose of being baptized in water is a testimony of repentance from sin and profession of faith.

> *I indeed baptize you with water **unto repentance**.*
> MATTHEW 3:11 NKJV

When we are baptized into the body of Christ:

The Holy Spirit is the agent of this baptism. John could not, nor any other believer cannot, perform this baptism. This is a work that only the Holy Spirit can do.

> *For as the body is one and has many members, but all the members of that one body, being many, are one body, so also is Christ. **For by one Spirit we were all baptized into one body**—whether Jews or Greeks, whether slaves or free—and have all been made to drink into one Spirit.*
> 1 CORINTHIANS 12:12-13 NKJV

Every believer is baptized by the Holy Spirit into the Body of Christ when they are saved. The purpose of this baptism is unity and fellowship with other believers.

When we are baptized with the Holy Spirit:

It is only Jesus who can be the agent of this baptism. The Holy Spirit cannot be the agent because He is the element. Jesus is the one who baptizes believers with the Holy Spirit.

> *I (John) indeed baptize you with water unto repentance, but He who is coming after me is mightier than I, whose sandals I am not worthy to carry.* ***He (Jesus) will baptize you with the Holy Spirit and fire.*** MATTHEW 3:11 NKJV

The baptism with the Holy Spirit happens when the Holy Spirit comes upon us and fills us.

> *Once when He was eating with them, He commanded them, "Do not leave Jerusalem until the Father sends you the gift He promised, as I told you before. John baptized with water, but in just a few days* **you will be baptized with the Holy Spirit.***"* ACTS 1:4-5 NLT

The purpose of Jesus baptizing us with the Holy Spirit is for spiritual power, which equips us for holy living. The Holy Spirit gives us anointing power, which equips us for effective service and a life that glorifies God.

> *But* **you shall receive power** *when the Holy Spirit has come upon you; and you shall be witnesses to Me in Jerusalem, and in all Judea and Samaria, and to the end of the earth.* ACTS 1:8 NKJV

THE FILLING WITH THE HOLY SPIRIT

When we read the account of Jesus baptizing His followers with the Holy Spirit on the Day of Pentecost, we discover that two things happened simultaneously. One is that the Holy

Spirit came upon them *outwardly* (Acts 1:8, Acts 2:1-3); the other is that the Holy Spirit filled them *inwardly* (Acts 2:4).

Although the baptism with the Holy Spirit and the filling of the Holy Spirit happened at the same time, each represents a different aspect and ministry of the Holy Spirit in our lives. We can see these two different aspects in the life of Jesus as well.

At the Jordan River, The Holy Spirit came **upon** Jesus.

> *And John bore witness, saying, "I saw the Spirit descending from heaven like a dove, and He remained **upon** Him."*
> JOHN 1:32 NKJV

Jesus was also **filled with** the Holy Spirit and then led by the Spirit into the wilderness.

> *Then Jesus, being **filled with** the Holy Spirit, returned from the Jordan and was led by the Spirit into the wilderness.*
> LUKE 4:1 NKJV

This two-fold ministry represents the work of the Holy Spirit in power and fullness. It is vital to our spiritual witness and our spiritual walk. The Holy Spirit coming upon us is for the purpose of anointing and empowering; the Holy Spirit filling us is for the purpose of enabling us to walk as Jesus walked and being conformed to His image. (I John 2:6, Romans 8:29).

There is another way we can understand the differences between these two ministries of the Holy Spirit in our lives. When the Holy Spirit is poured out *upon us*, it is a one-time experience that does not need to be repeated. The filling of the Holy Spirit within us is a life-long process, where we keep on being filled. Another way to say it is, "One baptism and many fillings."

Be filled with the Spirit. EPHESIANS 5:18 NKJV

In Ephesians 5:18, God makes it clear what His will is for each of His children. We are commanded to be filled with the Spirit. This verse can be translated from the original Greek text to mean, "Be filled, *and keep on being filled*, with the Holy Spirit."

The reason God's will is so clearly stated in this passage is because this is God's way of doing His work in us and through us. God is glorified in our lives when we have been emptied of ourselves and filled with Him. It is the one who is filled with the Holy Spirit who will do God's work, in God's way, at God's time, in God's place, and for God's glory.

A vessel can have water in it, but not be filled to the brim. A vessel can be filled to the brim, but not overflow. The Spirit-filled life is an abundant life that fills us to the brim and overflows to touch the lives of others. When we are filled with the Holy Spirit, He is in control of our lives and flows out through us like rivers of living water.

When He is in control, we still have our thoughts, feelings, and will, but we are no longer ruled by them. We have moods but we are not moody, we have thoughts but we are not thoughtless, we have choices, but we do not make them independently of His wisdom and will. Every area of our inner-life, including our attitudes and motives, are subject to the leading, authority, and guidance of the Holy Spirit.

When we are filled with the Holy Spirit we are freed from the bondage of being "full of ourselves." The Spirit-filled life joyfully proclaims, "It is no longer I who live, but Christ." It is a life that is continuously exploring and discovering the riches that are in Christ—we are free to love as He loves, give as He gives, and bless as He blesses.

The Fullness of the Holy Spirit

The Spirit-filled life is a holy and sanctifying life. It is a life that is in the world, but set apart. It is a life that can still be tempted, but it is a life where sin no longer has dominion. It is a life that faces opposition, spiritual warfare, trials, and persecution, but conquers, and is victorious, finding its strength in the joy of the Lord.

The Spirit-filled life is one of truest worship and deepest adoration. It brings music to our hearts and puts praise upon our lips. It brings forth a melody of psalms and spiritual songs, even songs in the darkest of nights.

The Spirit-filled life is an attractive life that is lived in the light of His approval. It is in full cooperation with the Holy Spirit's work as He shapes, forms, and conforms us to the image of Jesus Christ. It is a life of spiritual fruit and fragrance, of a pleasing disposition and right attitudes, and of pure motives and abundant grace.

The Spirit-filled life is one that is sensitive to not quenching or grieving the Holy Spirit, that turns its ear to listen to the Spirit's voice, and that fixes its heart to quickly and willingly respond to the Spirit's prompting.

The Spirit-filled life means that we are as dependent upon the Holy Spirit as Jesus was…in all things, in all ways, and at all times.

"The Spirit-filled must be Spirit-ruled. Those who are greatly used of God have no monopoly of the Holy Spirit; they are mighty through God because the Spirit has a monopoly on them." (Taken from the book *The Way to Pentecost* by Samuel Chadwick.)

His will for us is not to be empty, but full; not to be defeated, but victorious; not to be timid, but bold; not to be fearful, but to be strong in the Lord and in the power of His might.

> *This is the word of the LORD to Zerubbabel: "Not by might nor by power, but by My Spirit," says the LORD of hosts.*
> ZECHARIAH 4:6 NKJV

The Fullness of the Holy Spirit

My Prayer

God, Your work is so amazing!

You always do exceedingly above

all I could ever ask or think.

Thank You for the water of baptism

where I can publicly profess my faith

and let the whole world know that Jesus saves.

Thank You for the baptism by Your Holy Spirit

that has placed me into the Body of Christ

and made me a part of Your family.

Thank You for the baptism with the Holy Spirit

and for the spiritual power to live a dynamic life.

Thank You that the Holy Spirit has come

to equip me and fill me.

All glory and praise to You

for Your amazing generosity.

Amen.

*If you then, being evil,
know how to give good gifts to your children,
how much more will your heavenly Father
give the Holy Spirit to those who ask Him!*

LUKE 11:13 NKJV

CHAPTER 14

Receiving the Fullness of the Holy Spirit

The promised gift of the Holy Spirit is God's provision for us as His children. His fullness is a promise to be claimed and a gift to be received. There are many people mentioned in the New Testament who had the experience of being filled with the Holy Spirit.

> John, the son of Zacharias [Luke 1:15]
>
> Elizabeth, the mother of John [Luke 1:41]
>
> Jesus Christ [Luke 4:1]
>
> Jesus' disciples [Acts 2:1-4]
>
> About 120 in The Upper Room, including Mary and the brothers of Jesus [Acts 1:12-14]
>
> Believers and companions of Peter and John [Acts 4:23-31]
>
> The seven chosen to serve tables, including Stephen [Acts 6:3, 5-6]
>
> Saul [Acts 9:10-17]

Cornelius and all who were gathered in his house [Acts 10:24-46]

Barnabas [Acts 11:24]

The persecuted disciples [Acts 13:48-52]

Jesus said in John 7:37-39 that the gift of the Holy Spirit was for the thirsty—those who are thirsty for rivers of living water, thirsty for righteousness, thirsty for intimacy with God, thirsty for the power of God, thirsty for the glory of God, thirsty of the fullness of God's Spirit.

As the deer longs for streams of water, so I long for You, O God. PSALM 42:1 NLT

Spiritual thirst is longing after God. It is a need within us that we must have God and no substitute. Just like our body needs water and must drink, so our spirit needs God's presence and we must drink of His Spirit.

A thirsty person is not passive or indifferent about his need for water. A thirsty person does not need to analyze water, study water, or debate water—the need of a thirsty person is to drink water.

Each of us needs to personally appropriate the promise and the provision that Jesus has given us in the Holy Spirit. No one can drink for you. When you are thirsty, drinking is an uncomplicated thing to do. Drinking is so simple that even a newborn baby can do it. Jesus did not say, "If anyone thirsts let him come to Me and *think*." You cannot think your way into God's fullness, you must *drink* your way to fullness.

Are you spiritually thirsty? If you are, then Jesus promises to give you drink. No one needs to be spiritually dehydrated or die of spiritual thirst. This is Jesus' promise.

> *Blessed are those who hunger and thirst for righteousness, for they shall be filled.* MATTHEW 5:6 NKJV

Do you desire to drink of the rivers of living water that Jesus wants to pour out upon you? Come to Jesus, the One who will baptize you and fill you with the Holy Spirit. He has promised to satisfy your thirst and place within you the river of the Holy Spirit that will never run dry.

> *On the last day, that great day of the feast, Jesus stood and cried out, saying, "If anyone thirsts, let him come to Me and drink. He who believes in Me, as the Scripture has said, out of his heart will flow rivers of living water." But this He spoke concerning the Spirit, whom those believing in Him would receive; for the Holy Spirit was not yet given, because Jesus was not yet glorified.* JOHN 7:37-39 NKJV

Receiving the baptism and filling with the Holy Spirit is not difficult.

FIRST, prepare your heart to receive:

Confess and forsake all known sin.

> *He who covers his sins will not prosper, but whoever confesses and forsakes them will have mercy.*
> PROVERBS 28:13 NKJV

It is important for us to be a clean vessel when we drink of the Holy Spirit. A personal friend, who was thirsty for the baptism with the Holy Spirit, went before the Lord to receive. However, the Lord made it clear that his heart was not ready. The Lord reminded him of a sin he had carried against a former acquaintance. He knew he must first make things right. The following week he contacted his former acquaintance and asked for forgiveness. A few days later, after being reconciled with his friend, he prayed once again to receive the baptism with the Holy Spirit. This time his heart was clean and he freely drank of the rivers of living water that Jesus poured out upon him.

Give yourself fully to the Lord.

> *Dear brothers and sisters, I plead with you to give your bodies to God because of all He has done for you. Let them be a living and holy sacrifice—the kind He will find acceptable. This is truly the way to worship Him.* ROMANS 12:1 NLT

Not only do we need to release to the Lord anything we have been hanging on to, but we need to place our entire lives into His hands. It is through our full surrender that we will be free to move unhindered in His will and purposes for our lives. A boat is made to sail the sea, but as long as it is tied to the dock, even by a single cord, it is not free to move about the waters.

Set your heart on obedience.

> *We are His witnesses to these things, and so also is the Holy Spirit whom God has given to those who obey Him.*
> ACTS 5:32 NKJV

Hold no pre-conditions in your heart. Don't say to the Holy Spirit, "I will go here, but not there; I will do this, but not that." The Holy Spirit is not surrendering Himself to your will, but you are surrendering yourself to His will. There is no reason to fear or hold back. The Holy Spirit brings to your life everything that is agreeable and acceptable to the will of God. He will come, not to empower you to go your own way, but to go God's way—the good way, the right way, the best way, the highest way.

Receiving the Fullness of the Holy Spirit

Now, receive the baptism and filling with the Holy Spirit by faith.

> *That we might receive the promise of the Spirit through faith.* GALATIANS 3:14 NKJV

You receive God's gifts, not by striving but by trusting; not by working but by believing; not through fret, but through faith. Receiving the baptism and filling with the Holy Spirit is as simple as drinking water. If you are thirsty, drink. You drink by receiving His promise by faith.

As you prepare your heart to pray, ask the Holy Spirit to show you if there is any sin you need to repent of and confess. As you do, receive the cleansing of the blood of Jesus and His forgiveness.

The following prayer is simply suggested, it is not the perfect prayer, nor the only way you can pray. The important thing is to pray in faith, to pray from your heart, and to receive (drink) the fullness of the Holy Spirit from Jesus.

Ask Jesus now to baptize and fill you with the promised Holy Spirit...

My Prayer

Lord, with a heart washed clean through the blood of **Jesus**, I come to You to be baptized and filled with the **Holy Spirit**. I present myself fully to You, as a yielded vessel, to obey and glorify You. Use me as it pleases You.

I come to You unconditionally. I come to You thirsty. I come to drink. I come by faith, trusting in Your promise to baptize and fill me with the **Holy Spirit**. Thank You for Your promise and for the gift of the **Holy Spirit**.

Jesus, I ask You to baptize and fill me now with the **Holy Spirit** in this moment. By faith and with gratitude, I receive Your gift. **Holy Spirit**, I drink of You.

Jesus, thank You for baptizing me with the **Holy Spirit**. **Holy Spirit**, thank You for filling me with Your presence, and for coming upon me with Your power.

Amen.

Notes

¹⁶*And I will pray the Father,
and He will give you another Helper,
that He may abide with you forever—*

¹⁷*the Spirit of truth, whom the world cannot receive,
because it neither sees Him nor knows Him;
but you know Him, for He dwells with you
and will be in you.*

JOHN 14:16-17 NKJV

CHAPTER 15

Expectations

Receiving the baptism with the Holy Spirit does not mean you have arrived at a place of perfection or instant spiritual maturity. It is not the end of something, but rather the beginning of a deeper and richer walk with God.

Once you have received the gift of the baptism with the Holy Spirit you may think, *"Now what?"*

While this experience does have a starting point in your life, it does not have an ending point. God promises to complete the good work that He began in you throughout your life by bringing you to a place of spiritual maturity in your walk of faith and obedience.

Many changes will come into your walk with the Lord as a result of the baptism with the Holy Spirit.

What WILL happen:

The following will help you understand the deeper work taking place within you when you receive the baptism and filling with the Holy Spirit. Each area is based upon the fruit that became evident in the lives of those who were baptized and filled with the Holy Spirit throughout the book of Acts, including Peter and the Apostle Paul.

> **You will** grow in gladness of heart, in thankfulness, and gratitude for who you are in Christ and what it means to have Him at the center of who you are and all you do.
>
> **You will** begin a more consistent walk in the Spirit, become more sensitive to His leading and prompting, and more responsive to His voice.
>
> **You will** gain more ground in living a life of victory over sin, the enemy, and the flesh.
>
> **You will** more confidently draw upon His strength to overcome temptation.
>
> **You will** delight in the joys of being filled with the Spirit and empty of yourself.
>
> **You will** rest more deeply in the control of the Holy Spirit knowing that He is not only resident within you, but also president over you in the daily issues of life.
>
> **You will** long to do the things that please Him instead of doing what pleases you.
>
> **You will** move more purposefully, going at His pace and according to His plan.
>
> **You will** minister with greater boldness, spiritual authority, and power.
>
> **You will** experience new depths in worship, in prayer, and in your intimacy with the Lord.

Expectations

Our understanding is flawed if we think that once we are saved and filled with the Spirit that life will become easy, things will go our way, and our trials and hardships will be over. In fact, we can count on the opposite being true.

It is good to remember that after Jesus was baptized with the Holy Spirit in the Jordan River, He was led by the Holy Spirit into the wilderness for forty days where He was tempted and tested by the devil. The remaining time He spent on Earth was filled with hardships, opposition, persecution, and rejection by many.

The fruit of being filled with the Holy Spirit is not about popularity or fame. It does not mean you will be appreciated or celebrated, have a "big" ministry, become wealthy, or be given positions of power.

What WILL NOT happen:

The following will help you to understand what will NOT happen within you when you receive the baptism and filling with the Holy Spirit.

You will not become perfect (flawless) or arrive at a place where it is impossible to sin. After the disciples were all baptized with the Holy Spirit on the Feast of Pentecost, there were still issues that needed to be dealt with, problems to solve, exhortations that needed to be given, guidance that needed to be sought, disagreements that needed to be recognized, and various other issues that needed clarity and instruction within the body of Christ.

You will not become instantly mature in your spiritual growth. You will continue to grow in your walk and be pruned, be disciplined, and be shaped by the Holy Spirit as He continues the process of sanctifying and conforming you to the image of Jesus.

YOU WILL NOT enter into a life of spiritual ease (not to be confused with spiritual rest). Problems will not vanish; Satan will not stop his resistance and warfare; all of your stop-lights will not suddenly turn green; testing and trials will not cease. You will still need to resist, pray, believe, trust, endure hardships, fight the good fight, and overcome.

The Holy Spirit is your atmosphere.

The Holy Spirit not only lives in you, but you are to live in the Holy Spirit. Like a bird flies in the air, so you are made to "mount up with wings" and soar in the atmosphere of the Holy Spirit. God has intended for you to be as comfortable with your life in the Spirit as a bird is with its life in the air. A life in the Spirit means that you are "at home" in His presence, just as a fish is at home in the water. You could not imagine your life in Christ to be any other way.

> *The Spirit of truth, whom the world cannot receive, because it neither sees Him nor knows Him; but you know Him, for He dwells with you and will be in you. I will not leave you orphans; I will come to you. A little while longer and the world will see Me no more, but you will see Me. Because I live, you will live also. At that day you will know that I am in My Father, and you in Me, and I in you.... Jesus answered and said to him, "If anyone loves Me, he will keep My word; and My Father will love him, and* **We will come to him and make Our home with him.**" JOHN 14:17-20, 23 NKJV

There is a life for us to live and a path for us to follow, but it is His life that will be lived through us, and it is His path that will guide our steps. It won't be the path of least resistance, but it will be the right path, the good way, and the one that God's light shines upon with His approval.

The Holy Spirit has been symbolically identified as a dove, but the Holy Spirit is not a dove that can be kept locked up in a cage. We cannot put our controls upon the work and ministry of the Holy Spirit. We do not control Him, He controls us—this is the significance of a Spirit-filled life.

The Holy Spirit also invites us out of our own cages. Sometimes it is hard to come out of our cages, because we have lived there so long. Our cages have become our safe place. In our cages we have a sense of control, we know what to expect, and we become comfortable with the idea of life without any big surprises. But the Holy Spirit has come to release us, to free us, to take us on new adventures, to climb new heights, and to explore new depths.

We have nothing to fear about coming out of our cages, because we have nothing to fear about the Holy Spirit—He will surprise us, but He will never terrify us; He will delight us, but He will never defile us; He will stretch us, but He will never deceive us; He will edify us, but He will not exploit us. There is nothing in His character that would ever alarm us, disappoint us, confuse us, abuse us, misuse us, or belittle us.

The Holy Spirit brings peace, not passivity; joy, not silliness; decency, not embarrassment; control, not disorderliness; uprightness, not outrageousness; righteousness, not rudeness. The Holy Spirit always responds with the right behavior, speaks with the right words, responds with the right answer, works with the right motives, and only does what is in complete agreement with the will of God.

Expect a Personal Experience

When we read through the Book of Acts we find that the experiences of those who received the baptism and filling with the Holy Spirit were not always the same. There is no rule that your experience must be identical to someone else's in order to be genuine. We do not need to seek the same circumstances or the same manifestations of the baptism with the Holy Spirit that others have had. *Each believer's experience will be uniquely different.*

The important thing is to receive the gift of the Holy Spirit by faith. The experience you have with the Holy Spirit, the spiritual gifts He gives you, and how He chooses to manifest Himself in your life will be personal to you and according to His will.

Many people have had different experiences after receiving the baptism and filling with the Holy Spirit. These people had different temperaments and personalities, many had different church backgrounds, some immediately experienced a manifestation of a certain spiritual gift, others experienced a manifestation of certain spiritual gifts months or years later, some became very excited and full of joy, some became very quiet and filled with peace, some were set free of certain fears, and some were set free from certain bondages, yet they all had one thing in common—their experience was *real*.

Expect Spiritual Gifts

Spiritual gifts are not natural talents or human abilities. They are supernatural in origin. Spiritual gifts come from the Holy Spirit and are expressed through God's people, the body of Christ. The Holy Spirit is the Lord of all spiritual gifts. He alone manifests His gifts through us according to His will, not ours.

Expectations

> *But one and the same Spirit works all these things, distributing to each one individually as He wills.*
> 1 CORINTHIANS 12:11 NKJV

All spiritual gifts are grace gifts. We don't "earn" spiritual gifts, and they are not given by the Holy Spirit as awards for certain achievements on our part.

Each of us has the same Holy Spirit (this helps us understand our unity as believers), yet our individual spiritual gifts will not all be the same, be used in the same way, or produce the same results (this helps us understand our diversity as believers).

> *There are diversities of gifts, but the same Spirit. There are differences of ministries, but the same Lord. And there are diversities of activities, but it is the same God who works all in all.* 1 CORINTHIANS 12:4-6 NKJV

God does not want us to have a passive attitude regarding spiritual gifts, nor a "take it or leave it" approach. It grieves Him if we ignore what He has provided for us, if we discredit it, or if we want to pick and choose what we think is best for us.

> *And do not grieve the Holy Spirit of God, by whom you were sealed for the day of redemption.* EPHESIANS 4:30 NKJV

God's will for us is to pursue love, to earnestly desire the spiritual gifts of the Holy Spirit, and to use the gifts the Holy Spirit gives us to help build up His people.

God does not want us to have a puffed up attitude regarding spiritual gifts. One gift does not make someone better than another, nor does one gift make someone inferior to another. Spiritual gifts have been given by the Holy Spirit to benefit all.

God has ordained that the body of Christ be dependent upon one another, and bound together in love.

> *Pursue love, and desire spiritual gifts.*
> 1 CORINTHIANS 14:1 NKJV

We can be at peace knowing that there are no bad spiritual gifts. The Holy Spirit has not made a mistake regarding any gift. Every gift of the Holy Spirit should bless us and amaze us, whether we have that gift or not.

We do not need to fight, resist, question, debate, fear, or doubt what the Holy Spirit wills to do in our lives. He is God, and He is good; everything He does is righteous. Every gift that comes from the Holy Spirit is given for a good reason and a good purpose. He has not come to entertain or amuse us, but to work in us that which is pleasing in God's sight. The Holy Spirit who manifests the fruits that we all celebrate and desire, is the same Holy Spirit who manifests the spiritual gifts that we should all celebrate and desire.

Be Aware of Misuse and Counterfeits

Anything that is real can have a counterfeit, and anything that has a proper use can be used improperly. The only reason counterfeit money is printed is because real money exists. If someone tried to create a nine dollar bill in the United States, no one would accept it because a nine dollar bill does not exist. However, a ten dollar counterfeit bill might be accepted by an untrained eye.

In some countries, banks train their workers to identify counterfeits by having them study the markings of the original. When the workers become completely familiar with all the details of the original, spotting a counterfeit becomes easy.

Regarding the misuse of spiritual gifts, we need to be wise and discerning. Everything that claims to be of God may not always be genuine. God does not want us to be gullible and undiscerning. He wants us to be wise and able to recognize warning signs of false teaching. The enemy does work as an angel of light to deceive, and unfortunately, people do make false claims for personal gain. But if we apply the same principal strategy of the banks by studying the Bible and knowing the Scriptures well, we will be able to spot misuse of spiritual gifts.

Often, when spiritual gifts are being discussed among believers, someone will recall a negative experience they had or convey a story they have heard about how a spiritual gift was misused. Some accounts may be genuine and others may be overly exaggerated. Either way, we shouldn't let misuse or abuse keep us from what God has given us for our good and edification. The answer to misuse should never be non-use.

> *Do not despise prophecies. Test all things; hold fast what is good.* 1 THESSALONIANS 5:20-21 NKJV

> *Let two or three people prophesy, and **let the others evaluate what is said**. But if someone is prophesying and another person receives a revelation from the Lord, the one who is speaking must stop. In this way, all who prophesy will have a turn to speak, one after the other, so that **everyone will learn and be encouraged**. Remember that people who prophesy are in control of their spirit and can take turns. For **God is not a God of disorder but of peace**, as in all the meetings of God's holy people.* 1 CORINTHIANS 14:29-33 NLT

> *Beloved, do not believe every spirit, but **test the spirits**, whether they are of God; because many false prophets have gone out into the world.* 1 JOHN 4:1 NKJV

Below is a list of Scriptures to help you have a Godly attitude toward spiritual gifts while also being wise and discerning.

> Don't be ignorant of spiritual gifts. [1 Corinthians 12:1]
>
> Desire spiritual gifts. [1 Corinthians 12:31, 14:1]
>
> Do not forbid any gift. [1 Corinthians 14:39]
>
> Do not despise any gift. [1 Thessalonians 5:20]

Today, we do not need to seek the exact *circumstances* or *manifestations* of the experience of the baptism with the Holy Spirit that is recorded in the second chapter of Acts, but rather the *reality* of this experience through faith. In that chapter, we read about the outpouring of the Holy Spirit on the Jewish Feast of Pentecost.

Author and pastor, Samuel Chadwick, explained their experience in his book, *The Way to Pentecost*:

> "The day of Pentecost brought light, power, joy. There came to each illumination of mind, assurance of heart, intensity of love, fullness of power, exuberance of joy... no one needed to ask if they had received the Holy Spirit. Fire is self-evident. So is power."

This baptism with the Holy Spirit came upon a group of followers of Jesus Christ who were gathered in an upper room in Jerusalem. The book of Acts covers over 30 years of the Holy Spirit's working. During those years, no group or individual received the baptism with the Holy Spirit in exactly the same way as those in The Upper Room. Each experience came under different circumstances and had different manifestations. (The closest came at the house of Cornelius when the Holy Spirit was poured out upon the Gentile believers.)

In order for us to be baptized with the Holy Spirit today, we do not need to be in Jerusalem in an upper room, hear a mighty rushing wind, or see tongues of fire. The circumstances and momentary manifestations of the Holy Spirit will vary from person-to-person, but the reality of the experience is for a lifetime.

My Prayer

This final prayer is taken from the book of Ephesians and put into a personalized format.

I bow my knees to You,

the **Father** of our **Lord Jesus Christ**,

from whom the whole family in Heaven and Earth is named,

that You would grant me, according to the riches

of Your glory, to be strengthened with might

through **Your Spirit** in my inner man,

that **Christ** may dwell in my heart through faith;

that I, being rooted and grounded in love,

may be able to comprehend with all the saints

what *is* the width and length and depth and height—

to know the love of **Christ** which passes knowledge;

that I may be filled with all the fullness of **God**.

[EPHESIANS 3:14-19 NKJV]

Amen.

Notes

SECTION V

AUTHOR REFLECTIONS

CHAPTER 16

LEARNING THE WAYS OF THE HOLY SPIRIT

I am using this closing chapter to share with you some personal moments from my own life that tell how, as a lifelong student in the school of the Holy Spirit, I began to hear His voice and learn His ways. The Holy Spirit has been sent to teach each believer, each believer has been enrolled into His school, and each believer has their own story to tell. I hope these experiences from my own walk will be an encouragement to you in your life as you discover the person, the purpose, and the power of the promised Holy Spirit.

ROY LESSIN

THE SIMPLICITY OF IT ALL

> *But without faith it is impossible to please Him, for he who comes to God must believe that He is, and that He is a rewarder of those who diligently seek Him.*
> HEBREWS 11:6 NKJV

Ask, and it will be given to you; seek, and you will find; knock, and it will be opened to you. MATTHEW 7:7 NKJV

One of the most amazing things to me about the work and ministry of the Holy Spirit in our lives is not His complexity, but His simplicity. He doesn't knock us over with big words, or speak to us with a vocabulary we don't understand. He is always clear and specific. He never leaves us in confusion. When it comes to the working of the Kingdom of God in our lives, I believe that the Holy Spirit moves us toward simplicity.

Think for a moment about the words in Scripture that bring the riches of His Kingdom to us—trust, believe, receive, drink, eat, follow, and ask.

When I was a young believer, I can remember how easy the things of God came to me. When I read something in the Bible, I believed it. If I had a need, I trusted God to meet it. When I uttered a prayer, I knew God heard it and that He would answer. This child-like expectancy of faith never needs to change as we grow and mature in the Lord. The more we trust Him, the more we should trust Him more. He never changes, why should we?

In my own experience, I had no immediate manifestation of the Holy Spirit. At the time, I was sick and in bed. I had been seeking the baptism with the Holy Spirit for several months, but without result. While in bed, I picked up a book to read. I discovered it had a chapter on the Holy Spirit and turned to it. As I began reading the chapter, I found an illustration that helped turn on a light of understanding. I realized I had been attempting to make something very complicated that Jesus had made very simple. I had been trying so hard to receive that I had failed to see that the baptism with the Holy Spirit was Jesus' free gift to me if I would simply receive it by faith.

That day, in the summer of 1962, as a first year student in Bible College, I got out of bed and knelt in prayer. By faith, with a short and simple prayer, I asked and *received* from Jesus, the baptism with the Holy Spirit. There was no emotion, no spiritual gift, or any other manifestation that followed my prayer, but I knew I had received and the matter was settled in my heart (The reality of what I had received from Jesus that day has remained with me now for over 50 years).

The next day, at a student chapel service, I stood and shared the following, "Yesterday, in my room, I knelt in prayer and received the baptism with the Holy Spirit." That was the end of my testimony. There was nothing else to share…but a surprise was coming!

Two days later, I had an unexpected and deeply moving manifestation of the Holy Spirit. I was at work, operating a machine, when suddenly waves of joy began pouring over me. Wave followed wave. I was caught up and filled up with joy. Pure joy. Not the joy of circumstance, or the joy of good news, but the joy of the Holy Spirit's presence…nothing else was needed to produce this joy, just Him. I walked in the special manifestation of His joy for about two weeks. After the two weeks, the joy of the Lord didn't leave my life, but the unique manifestation of joy that I had experienced began to subside. This outpouring of joy happened only once.

What will your experience be like? It may be something like my own experience, or it may be something very different. When Charles Finney speaks about His experience with the Holy Spirit, he describes waves of love coming over him, so deep and intense that Finney did not know if he could contain it. In all the experiences I have read from others who have received the baptism with the Holy Spirit, I have never read one quite like Finney's.

The counsel I would give you is not to seek a specific gift or a certain type of experience, but to seek the Giver, Jesus Christ. Receive by faith the gift of the Holy Spirit…then let Him have His way with you without resistance, and doubting nothing.

The "I Care" Attitude

Your ears shall hear a word behind you, saying, "This is the way, walk in it," Whenever you turn to the right hand or whenever you turn to the left. ISAIAH 30:21 NKJV

My sheep hear My voice, and I know them, and they follow Me. JOHN 10:27 NKJV

The first time I remember the voice of the Holy Spirit speaking to me in a personal way happened during my first year in Bible School. I had only been a believer for a short time when I left Southern California and headed for Bethany Fellowship in Minnesota. It was early January when I arrived and the change in climate was a shock! Snow was everywhere and the temperature was in the low teens. Over the next few months it would have been an understatement to say that I needed to adjust to Bethany, and Bethany needed to adjust to me.

One of the things that I brought to Bethany from Southern California was a casual lifestyle and an attitude that said "I couldn't care less." I soon discovered that God's Kingdom did not operate under such an attitude. Somehow, by the grace of God, I survived the winter and made it to spring. It felt great to be outside again without a jacket and boots. The warming air and the budding trees revived me.

During one warm spring afternoon, I stopped in at the student store and picked up a candy bar. I was walking past the girls' dorm when I took my last bite. I wadded up the empty paper wrapping and tossed it to the ground. Before I could take two steps, I heard a still small voice speaking to my heart, "Pick up the paper and put it in the trash can."

"That's ridiculous," I thought, and walked on. After about two steps, the voice of the Holy Spirit spoke the same words to me again. My response was the same, and I continued walking. Once again, I heard that same gentle voice speaking to my heart for a third time. "OK," I finally responded, "I'll do it." I turned around, walked back to the wadded up paper and put it in the trash can.

With all the major issues that were going on in the world at that time, and with all the problems and needs that faced God's people, why would He talk to *me* about picking up a candy wrapper? I soon learned that even though my attitude toward life was "I couldn't care less," God's attitude was, "I care." He wanted me to pick up that wrapper because He wanted to begin to build a caring attitude in me, not just for candy wrappers, but for all things. Another thing I learned through that experience was that it was the beginning of a discipline of character that the Holy Spirit was bringing into my life.

It was not a discipline of heaviness or condemnation, but a discipline of hope, encouragement, and purpose. My obedience to His voice became a tiny but important step in learning how to allow the Holy Spirit to build that character of Jesus within me. The issue of picking up a candy wrapper soon moved to picking my clothes up off the floor and straightening out my desk drawer. At the end of two years, this discipline of the Holy Spirit lifted from my life. By this time, throwing candy wrappers or leaving my clothes on the floor were no longer issues.

Not doing these things became a part of me. The Holy Spirit, in His tender way, had woven these things into my character. It became a joy for me to be neat and to begin to carry an "I care, because God cares," attitude in my heart.

Trust Me for It

> Trust in the LORD with all your heart, and lean not on your own understanding; in all your ways acknowledge Him, and He shall direct your paths. PROVERBS 3:5-6 NKJV

> Commit your way to the LORD, trust also in Him, and He shall bring it to pass. PSALM 37:5 NKJV

I will always remember the time when my wife and I were newly married and temporarily living in the couples' dormitory at the Bible College we both graduated from a year earlier. I had returned to finish a class so that I could receive my diploma. One Sunday evening we were in our room writing letters. After we each completed a letter we realized that we didn't have any stamps. At that time, first class postage was a nickel. "All we need is ten cents," I told my wife, "Let's look around the room and see if we can come up with it."

We looked in the drawers, in our pants pockets, and in her purse. After our search was over we had managed to round up nine pennies. "All we need now is one penny," I responded, "I'll just go down the hall and borrow a penny from one of my friends. A penny should be an easy thing to borrow." A few moments later I approached the door of one of my friends. As I was about to knock, the still small voice of God's Spirit spoke to my heart, "Don't borrow the penny, trust Me for it instead." I returned to our room and told my wife of my decision not to borrow the penny, but to trust the Lord to provide it for us instead.

A few minutes later I stepped out into the dorm hallway and ran into one of the married students who had just returned from a trip downtown.

We chatted for about five minutes and throughout our visit I noticed that he kept playing with something between his fingers. When our conversation was over I asked him out of curiosity what it was that he had between his fingers. "Oh this," he answered, "It's just a penny. Here." And with that he flipped the penny in the air and into my palm. I stood there in amazement, gazing at that penny. I held the coin between my fingers and walked into our room.

When my wife looked at me, I lifted the hand that held the penny and showed it to her. We stood there overcome by the care of God for us, realizing that He loved us so much that He would even provide a penny. In such a simple and clear way, God showed us that He can be trusted, not only for the big things in our lives but also for the little things, down to the smallest detail. Through the years the Lord has led us into many experiences that have brought us back again and again to the importance of trusting God, in simple faith, to be our complete provider.

There are people who challenge us to work more, study more, witness more, and give more, but where are the challenges to trust more? It saddens me when I meet believers whose faith has grown colder through the years. Many have heard teaching that has caused them to question more instead of believe more. For some, their doctrines have led them into areas of unbelief, doubt, and skepticism. These areas are enemies and thieves that rob us of our true joys.

Yet, even when these enemies attack us, the tender ministry of the Holy Spirit continues to draw us back to the foundations of our faith, to the quiet waters of salvation, to the lowly place of worship, to the peace of His presence, to the simplicity of the cross, to the beauty of His face, and to the goodness of God to us in Jesus Christ.

> Have no fears or worries,
> Simply be at rest—
> Trusting in your Father,
> For He knows what is best.
> He is always faithful,
> Walking by your side—
> Through His tender mercies,
> His goodness will provide.
> Everything He's promised
> He will surely do—
> His eye is on the sparrow,
> And He watches over you.

The River

> On the last day, that great day of the feast, Jesus stood and cried out, saying, "If anyone thirsts, let him come to Me and drink. He who believes in Me, as the Scripture has said, out of his heart will flow rivers of living water." But this He spoke concerning the Spirit, whom those believing in Him would receive; for the Holy Spirit was not yet given, because Jesus was not yet glorified. JOHN 7:37-39 NKJV

> Fruit trees of all kinds will grow along both sides of the river. The leaves of these trees will never turn brown and fall, and there will always be fruit on their branches. There will be a new crop every month, for they are watered by the river flowing from the Temple. The fruit will be for food and the leaves for healing. EZEKIEL 47:12 NLT

In 1971, the Lord's path for my life brought me into a relationship with three other men who shared a common vision to make Christ known to our generation. Together we launched a Christian publishing company that would later come to be known as DaySpring Cards.

Through the gifting that God had given me, I spent most of my time in the creative area working on products and writing copy. Ideas would come, and we would publish them. Within a few years we were starting to develop a small line of Christian greeting cards. From that point on, the company began to grow rapidly. More and more of my time was spent writing and helping to develop our cards. Sixteen years passed and I was still doing most of the writing for our card lines. It was becoming more and more difficult to keep up with the growing demand. Things needed to change.

As the pressures began to build, it became apparent that I needed to lay some things down. One major thing that I had to release was the idea that I had to do all the writing for our cards. This was a burden that I had put upon myself. Because of my workload, and some other personal struggles that I was going through, I came to a place where I felt I had nothing left to give. Darkness and a sense of despair settled over me. I struggled for months wondering what I should do. Eventually I stepped out of the creative division of DaySpring and seriously considered leaving the company.

It was in that dark time that the Holy Spirit brought a new light of hope to my heart. He strengthened my faith and began to rebuild my courage to move on.

As I thought more about my future, some of the leadership of DaySpring asked me if I would be willing to do some work in the catalog division of our company. The division was called Best to You. At first, the idea had no appeal to me. I was about to turn it down when I heard the Holy Spirit speak these words to my heart, "Say yes. This is what I have for you." In 1991, without knowing why God was leading me to Best to You, I reported to work.

The job I was given was to write sales copy for the catalog, something I had never done. "If this is what you have for me Father," my heart prayed, "I will do it willingly and thankfully." Six months passed. I was starting to write copy for my second catalog when something completely unexpected happened. One of our marketing experts suggested that we develop a premium for the next catalog.

The suggestion for the premium was a devotional book, and they suggested that I write it. When the request to write the devotional book reached me, I was overjoyed. For years I had desired to write a devotional book for DaySpring, but the greeting card demands never allowed me to do it. God was truly granting me a desire of my heart. I accepted the project.

The next day at work I sat down in front of my computer to begin writing the book. When I looked up at my blank computer screen a sense of panic hit me. "Can I do this?" I wondered, "Do I really have anything to say?" After much hesitation, I took a step of faith and began to move my fingers across the keyboard. The more I typed the more the words came. At times I couldn't type fast enough. Within a few weeks the devotional book, *Always Loved, Never Forgotten* was completed. I was amazed!

During the time that I wrote my first devotional, God was resurrecting something creatively within me that I knew had died. It was at this time that He opened up my understanding to something that changed my entire outlook to the creative process. What God showed me was a beautiful, clear, wide, flowing river. The headwaters of the river began at the heart of God. The river was His Holy Spirit. "This is My creative river." He said, "It is an eternal river, for everything about Me is eternal. I am The Creator and my creativity is eternal."

My heart immediately responded to what God was showing me.

> "Father," I said. "What should I do?"
>
> "Get in," He replied.
>
> "How do I do that?" I asked.
>
> "By faith," He answered.
>
> "By faith?" I questioned, "Is it that simple?"
>
> "Yes." He replied, "It is that simple. Get in."

That day, by faith, I stepped into God's creative river.

When I stepped in, there were new things that I discovered. One was that the river immediately touched me. It washed, cleansed, refreshed, and renewed me.

There was something about the river that called me to remain there and to daily delight in its benefits.

The second thing I discovered was the vastness of the river. There was plenty of room for me to move about, and there was also an abundance of water for others. There was enough creative room for all who would come. I realized that I didn't have to feel like I had to "do it all." Instead, my creative interest was focused on what God was sending downstream to touch my life. There were things that God was also sending downstream that were intended for others. There was no competition in the river. This realization brought great freedom and liberty to my spirit.

A third thing I discovered was that the things God was sending downstream to touch my life were not meant for me alone. Each thing was meant to move downstream to touch the lives of others. I could not hold onto, or possess as mine, anything that God was giving me. I realized that creativity not only comes from God, but that the work is done by Him and goes back to Him. In the end, the glory is His. I found great freedom in not having to hold onto the things I did, nor did I have to defend them.

A final thing that I discovered was that there was no striving in the river, only a flow. I didn't have to try and make things happen. The flow was God's, not mine.

I knew that He alone was the source of all I did. This realization freed me from pressure, stress, and burn out.

My experience in God's river moved me to a new level of creativity, joy, and rest in the work that God had given me to do. A deeper trust in the Lord entered my heart; a fuller understanding of what God had called me to do entered my spirit; a new desire and expectation for how God would use me entered my vision. Each time I sat down to write there was a fresh sense of wonder as the river of God's Spirit tenderly began to reveal new things that He was sending my way.

About the Author

Roy Lessin has dedicated his life to ministry. For more than 50 years, he has been studying and teaching others what the Bible says about the Holy Spirit. His words have ministered to countless people over the years in a variety of personal and professional venues, most notably DaySpring Cards.

In 1971, Roy, along with three other Christian men started a Christian publishing company. After its first year in business, the company created a Christmas card with this message: "When you get right down to it, the only thing that really matters is Jesus." That card was the beginning of DaySpring Cards—a global leader in Christian cards, gifts, and inspirational products, and a subsidiary of the world's largest greeting card company, Hallmark. Roy spent many years at DaySpring in various creative and editorial roles bringing hope and encouragement to the body of Christ.

Today, Roy is an active Bible teacher and continues to be involved with DaySpring Cards, serving in various pastoral roles, consulting, and helping to create new products.

Recommended Reading

Deeper Experiences of Famous Christians by J. Lawson

Spiritual Power by D.L. Moody

The Person and Work of the Holy Spirit by R.A. Torrey

The Way to Pentecost by Samuel Chadwick

The Work of the Holy Spirit by Octavius Winslow

They Found the Secret by Raymond Edman

When He is Come by A.W. Tozer

Why God Used D.L. Moody by R.A. Torrey

Notes